AMERICA'S BEST BBQ
HOME-STYLE

AMERICA'S BEST BBQ

HOME-STYLE

What the Champions Cook in Their Own Backyards

Ardie A. Davis, PhB, and

Chef Paul Kirk, CWC, PhB, BSAS

Andrews McMeel
Publishing, LLC

Kansas City · Sydney · London

Andrews McMeel Publishing, LLC
an Andrews McMeel Universal company
1130 Walnut Street, Kansas City, Missouri 64106

www.andrewsmcmeel.com

13 14 15 16 17 SDB 10 9 8 7 6 5 4 3 2 1

ISBN: 978-1-4494-2768-9
Library of Congress Control Number: 2012950109

Book design by Diane Marsh

ATTENTION: SCHOOLS AND BUSINESSES
Andrews McMeel books are available at quantity discounts with bulk purchase for educational, business, or sales promotional use. For information, please e-mail the Andrews McMeel Publishing Special Sales Department: specialsales@amuniversal.com

For John Raven, PhB— The BBQ Icon

a.k.a. Daredevil Bad McFad, Commissioner of Barbecue

Contents

WE BUILT THIS ENTIRE BOOK ON ONE SIMPLE QUESTION:

WHAT DO CHAMPIONSHIP BARBECUERS COOK AT HOME IN THEIR OWN BACKYARDS, WHEN THERE ARE NO RULES BUT THE SIMPLE LAWS OF PHYSICS AND BASIC CHEMISTRY?

We got more than 100 delicious answers, along with tips and stories from the champions that will inform, entertain, and maybe even inspire you to take your next backyard cookout to a whole new level.

This book serves two purposes: introducing you to the champs and introducing you to some of the best barbecue you've ever eaten. You won't see most of the barbecue here on the judging tables at competitions. If you are lucky enough to befriend the team that gave us the recipe, however, you may get a bite if you are invited to socialize with the team in its booth at a contest. For many pros, their camper and booth become their home away from home during the barbecue season, and many booths take on a backyard feel as old friends and competitors come together to eat and swap stories. Most cooks will gladly share tips and recipes, especially when your interest is in backyard fare instead of contest secrets. Ask them questions about how to improve your backyard barbecue skills. And it's always fun to hear stories about backyard cooking disasters, especially because you can learn from their mistakes. A few of our favorites are on page 12.

We have written books on what the pros cook in their restaurants and on the competition circuit. This time we wanted to know what they cook when they don't have to follow strict rules or pay attention to profit margins and customer demand. This book is a gift to you from our many friends in the global barbecue community—champions and almost champions. It also demystifies them. Barbecue contest champions are everyday folk like you and us. They just took their backyard cooking beyond their backyard. Many say that at some point they were bitten by the barbecue bug and didn't look back, hooked on the fun and friendly atmosphere and hog wild for smoking meat throughout the night and the wee hours of the morning, all for a chance at points and prize money. While you may not seek those yourself, the recipes in this book will at least earn you the title of king or queen of the backyard cookout.

We'll be the first to say that some of the best barbecue is backyard barbecue. Contest rules and regulations literally put barbecue creativity in a box—a turn-in box. Failure to follow contest rules will disqualify an entry. Backyard cooks can be creative with no penalties. So while some of the recipes in this book are competition quality and comply with the rules, most are on the more

creative side. You'll wonder why champions ever care to cook to contest specifications when you try what they cook at home. We asked them, and you'll get a variety of answers in their tips and stories.

We have been involved in competition barbecue for more than thirty years each—Paul as a competitor with one of the most impressive win records in the world and Ardie as a contest organizer and a judge hundreds of times at world champion, state, regional, and local contests, including the Memphis in May World Champion Barbecue Cooking Contest, the Jack Daniel's World Championship Invitational Barbecue, and the National Capital Barbecue Battle. We've been there, done that, and are proud to call hundreds of barbecue champions all over the world our friends. Those friends are proud to share their experience with you.

Every year, about 1,000 barbecue contests are held all over the United States and Canada and throughout the world, and teams come from all over the globe to compete. Although we strived to make sure every region of the United States is represented in this book, the recipes are for the most part not regional specialties. Stuffed mushroom appetizers, for example, are as likely to show up at a backyard barbecue in

the shadow of Mount Rainier as in a backyard in suburban Maryland. Beans are one of the most likely dishes to show up at any backyard barbecue, though they can be prepared in a cornucopia of fantastic ways, such as in Paul Schatte's Head Country II Pinto Beans Cilantro Style. That doesn't mean the recipes in this book aren't creative, though. Far from it! One taste of Burnt Finger BBQ Bourbon Brie, Scottie Johnson's Shrimp-Stuffed Avocados with Citrus Aioli, or Chris Lilly's Flank Steak and Shiitake Yakitori and you'll know they're in a whole new league.

To add an international flavor, we asked some of our barbecue champ friends in Estonia, England, Puerto Rico, and Norway to share some recipes too. Thanks to Jaan Habicht, Jeremy Fowler, the BBQ Freaks (Jose Bengoa, Yolanda Bolivar, and Gabriel Antunez), and Craig Whitson, you can wow your guests with a touch of unusual backyard cuisine when you feel like serving something different—Jaan's Barbecue Meat "Cake," for example, or Craig Whitson's ElvisLaks Grilled Salmon.

Most of the recipes here are in the six-to-eight-servings range, by design. We scaled down some of the recipes that would serve an army, but we're talking about barbecue here. In our experience, people tend to eat more than usual

A perfect score in a Kansas City Barbeque Society sanctioned contest is 180. Of six judges, the scores of five count—the lowest is thrown out. Nine is the highest score a judge can give in each category.

So, 5 x 9 on Appearance = 45;
5 x 9 on Tenderness = 45;
5 x 9 on Taste = 45, doubled to 90
(because it's more important
than the other factors);
45 + 45 + 90 = 180.

when barbecue is on the table. Furthermore, if you're going to take the time and make the effort to prepare a great dish, especially if you're using best-quality ingredients, you'll want to make sure there is plenty for everyone—maybe even with a few leftovers. Feel free to adjust the quantities to serve more or fewer accordingly.

One bonus with the recipes in this book is that most are not complicated. Champs not only serve these dishes in their backyards; they also eat them at contests while they tend the fires, and unless they travel to contests in a home on wheels, they don't have all the equipment and convenience of the home kitchen. The ability to adapt is part of what made them champions.

As you read this book and try the recipes, imagine that our featured barbecue champs are right there with you, coaching you on how to make your backyard fare the best ever. They are with you all the way—from tips on choosing the best grill for your needs to essential tools and handy gadgets, food prep and presentation, and an array of recipes to make your backyard barbecues celebrations to remember! They will crank up the quality of your food, as well as your homestyle pitmaster reputation. Light the fire, bring out the meat, and grab your tongs. Let's get started!

WHAT IS BARBECUE?

There is no universal consensus. Barbecue is a method of cooking. Barbecued meat is also barbecue. A gathering of people to eat barbecue is a barbecue too.

CNN Money writer Paul R. La Monica metaphorically referred to a current U.S. economic situation as a "BBQ Recovery"—that is, "a slow and low rebound," an allusion to the slow and low method of barbecue cooking, which involves cooking meat at low temperatures (225° to 275°F) for several hours—from 4 to 24 or more. The result is meat that is tender and smoky, with about 25 percent of the original bulk lost through rendering of fat and juices, but percentages vary by meat and meat quality. When barbecue is called "smoking," the reference is to "hot smoking" in a barbecue pit, as opposed to "cold smoking," which involves cooking brined meats at a low temperature, usually for several days. Traditionally that is done in a smokehouse. Both methods impart smoke flavor to the meat.

The word *barbecue* is sometimes used interchangeably with *grilling*. Grilling is a method of cooking foods directly or indirectly over hot coals or flames for short periods of time, from a few seconds to more than an hour. Thus grilling is hot and fast; smoking is slow and low. Grilled or smoked, we call it barbecue.

Many barbecuers insist that grilling is not barbecue. We have no argument, however, with backyard cooks who invite friends and family to a "barbecue" featuring grilled hot dogs, sausages, steaks, or burgers. We'd gladly attend! While the folks on the barbecue circuit tend to favor their craft, and it's reflected in their recipes, more than a few like to grill at home so they can spend less time with their cooker and more time with their company. They, too, have provided some fast feasts from the flames so that you'll have a variety of choices for your next gathering.

CHAPTER 1: Beginners can save a lot of time, energy, and money by listening to basic advice from the champs, and seasoned backyard veterans might also learn a tip or two. After a combined total of at least 100 years of barbecue experience between us, one thing we know for sure is that, like all else in life, you never know it all—there's always more to learn.

When we asked the champs for backyard barbecue tips, a few commonsense constants emerged, plus some new ideas. We'll begin with the constants.

Backyard Barbecue Basics

COMMONSENSE BACKYARD BARBECUE BASICS

Put everything in its place. This culinary basic, coined in French as *mise en place*, is obvious and essential. Sometimes you can get by with forgetting something easy to fix, like herbed butter to finish your steaks. Other times you could be in big-time trouble if you forget to purchase an essential ingredient, thereby throwing off your timing.

Orchestrate everything. Boy Scout founder Lord Baden-Powell's motto, "Be prepared," was meant to apply to all aspects of living a responsible life, and pros will tell you it's also an essential culinary principle. Think ahead as to how you will orchestrate every detail of your backyard barbecue. Our backyard barbecue planning checklist on page 14 will help.

Befriend your local butcher. "Paul, Paul, it worked!" exclaimed an excited graduate of Chef Paul's pitmaster class. "I did the whole routine. Introduced myself to the butcher. Told him I'm getting into barbecue and need his help. Took home some ribs he recommended, smoked 'em, brought him a sample, and asked him why he had recommended those particular slabs. He told me how to pick the best slabs and said, from now on, just let him know when I'm going to barbecue and he'll set aside his best slabs for me." The late "Wild Man" Barry Martin was on a roll. He won at Grain Valley and, with two other students, garnered fifteen other awards.

Log it. Keep notes on each dish you cook. If you make changes, keep track. When dishes turn out to be exceptionally good, you'll be able to repeat them without any guesswork. When dishes are disappointing, check your notes for clues as to what went wrong or how to improve it the next time.

Gear, Gadgets, and Extras

On the circuit, the pros use a variety of cookers, from custom-made to commercially manufactured. Fifty-five-gallon drums made into cookers; cinder block pits—above or below ground—with grates and steel plates for lids; brick pits with carousel grates; "aquarium" pits with glass walls; stainless-steel pits fueled with gas, wood, electricity, or wood pellets; and large steel custom-made pits are what we've seen most often.

The barbecue industry is booming, with many companies offering grills that range from inexpensive to very expensive, but you don't need fancy or expensive equipment to cook like a pro. In fact, we know a backyard barbecuer in the Missouri Ozarks who gets by perfectly with a home-built pit made of cinder blocks, fencing, and an inverted steel wheelbarrow hood. It's not for everyone, but it'll do. If you don't already have a grill, we recommend starting with the low-tech and inexpensive icon of backyard cooking, the kettle grill. As competition barbecuer Donny Teel of Buffalo's Bar-B-Q tells us, "One of my favorite pieces of equipment is a 22½-inch Weber grill. You can buy one for $100 or less, and it works great for direct or indirect heat."

It's a good idea to think about and write down your barbecue lifestyle before choosing the best grill for your needs and your backyard. How often do you cook outdoors? What do you like to cook? How many people do you generally cook for? How much are you willing to spend, or does price matter? Knowing yourself, your wants, and your needs will lead you to making the best selection, and you may want to take your list of needs to a specialty barbecue store if you're buying your first grill.

Paul's standard advice is to figure out how and how many you are cooking for and get the cooker that's the next size up. The reason: you will get so hooked on how great your barbecue is that you will be throwing bigger parties. It's much cheaper to get the next size up than to buy two pits.

Finally, as Kelly and Roni Wertz of 4 Legs Up BBQ remind us, "Know your cooker. If you are getting a new smoker or grill for the big party, get it a few weeks or a month ahead of time. Practice those dishes on your new cooker so you will know what temperature they need to run at to make everything work in your time frame." Or, as Clint Cantwell of Smoke in Da Eye puts it, "Be one with the grill. The more you use it, the more comfortable you'll be trying items other than hamburgers and hot dogs on the grill. By knowing its hot spots, how temperatures react when you open and close the lid, and other nuances, you'll be cooking up grilled pizzas and rack of lamb in no time." And by all means, make sure to invite us over!

Charcoal Grills

The recipes in this book are from professionals, and they almost always use charcoal grills instead of gas, but you can use what you have and what you're comfortable with. The results may not be exactly the same, but you'll still end up with some great barbecue. Whatever you use, study the owner's manual for basic guidance and tips.

Charcoal grills are more affordable than gas grills, and they can reach higher temperatures. A charcoal grate holds coals on the bottom, and a grill rack above the coals holds the food. Vents on the bottom and in the lid help control temperature (on most models).

When cooking on a gas grill, bring depth of flavor by wrapping a handful of wood chips in a double layer of heavy-duty aluminum foil, poking a few holes in the foil, and placing the packet under the grates. The chips will slowly smolder, releasing flavorful smoke from this inexpensive "smoke bomb" while ensuring a quick cleanup.

–Clint Cantwell, Smoke in Da Eye

Charcoal grills are pretty easy to maintain. Keep the grill rack clean, and after the grill cools, remove the ashes to ensure proper air flow the next time you grill. When the grill is completely cool, wipe the inside and outside surfaces of the grill with a soft cloth and warm, soapy water. Rinse with clean water and wipe dry. To help protect the body from the weather and minimize white spots and oxidation, use a paper towel to apply a light coating of vegetable oil to the outside of the grill while it's cool. You can also buy a water-resistant cover to protect your grill when not in use.

Gas Grills

Gas grills are quick to preheat—10 to 15 minutes. Multiple burners allow you to control the heat better than a charcoal grill. Gas grills are also less messy—no charcoal or fire starters—and they burn longer than charcoal. One 20-pound tank lasts for 12 to 14 hours. It's easier to maintain higher temperatures on a gas grill than on a charcoal grill, but if you're cooking for long periods of time, you'll use a lot of gas.

Gas grills use lava rocks or ceramic briquettes. Ceramic briquettes don't burn completely as charcoal does. Lava rocks and metal plates are more similar alternatives to charcoal. Lava rocks can be used many times but eventually need to be replaced.

Simple maintenance adds years to the life of a gas grill. Check the gas fitting for leaks each time you connect and disconnect by using a mixture of soap and water. Bubbles indicate a leak. You'll also want to periodically check the tubes connecting the propane tank to the grill to ensure there are no cracks or holes. Regularly empty the grease catch pan to prevent flare-ups and fires. Store the tank outdoors, not in an enclosed space, and detached from the grill.

After every use, turn your grill on high for 10 to 15 minutes with the lid closed. Turn off the grill and let it cool slightly. Loosen the residue from the grill rack with a brass-bristle brush. This not only prevents sticking but also helps to prevent flare-ups. When the grill is completely cool, wipe the inside and outside surfaces of the grill with a soft cloth and warm, soapy water. Rinse with clean water and wipe dry.

An offset smoker is nice to have if you do a lot of smoking on your gas grill, but if you smoke food only occasionally, you can purchase an accessory metal smoker box, a small perforated metal container placed on a gas grill's lava rocks or ceramic briquettes to hold wood chips and provide smoke. If you don't want to purchase a smoker box, you can put soaked wood chips in heavy-duty foil, seal and poke holes in the top, and place on the hot briquettes, rocks, or coals.

Gadgets

Some say America is gadget-obsessed. If there's a problem that needs fixing, there's a gadget to fix it. Some would add that there are gadgets to fix problems that didn't exist before a gadget was created to fix it. Gadgets may or may not be an obsession, but they're here and they're strong. How do they play out in the world of championship barbecue—in contests and at home? They range from simple devices used to handle meat—flip it or grip it—to complex devices such as remote-control monitoring and adjustment equipment.

High-tech vs. low-tech separates the champs on the question of essential gear and gadgets. Then again, low-tech champs have been known to love their smart phone or iPad, but not be enamored of high-tech grilling gear and gadgetry. That said, the champs we talked with will allow that your backyard barbecue is more likely to be a success if you have the following items on hand:

- fire-starter chimney

- welder's or griller's gloves

MAKE THAT A CHIMNEY, NOT A CHIMINEA!

Before we competed in our first contest, the Bricktown in Oklahoma City, we went online to get a list of equipment we'd need. We bought everything on the list, including a chiminea, and hauled it to the contest. As luck would have it, we were assigned a space right next door to Mike and Debbie Davis of Lotta Bull BBQ—one of the winningest teams around! Talk about feeling intimidated. As it turned out, they were friendly and helpful and not intimidating at all once we got to know them. I noticed some puzzled looks on their faces when they glimpsed at our chiminea. We ended up not using the chiminea. At the end of the contest we loaded it up and took it home. Later, when I took another look at the equipment list we had used, I noticed it said "chimney," *not* "chiminea." After we got to know Mike and Debbie better, I told them the truth about the chiminea, and they haven't let us live that down yet!
—Darian Khosravi, Kosmo's Q

- thermometers—for your grill and for your meat

- long-handled tongs and spatulas

- basting mops and brushes

- spray bottles for basting meat and taming flare-ups

- drip pan

- water pan for smoking

- ABC fire extinguisher

- sharp knives

- cutting boards

There are essential gadgets and there are favorite gadgets. Here's what some of our champs said when asked to name their single favorite gadget:

Chris Capell, Dizzy Pig: The coolest gadget to come out in the last 15 years is the BBQ Guru (a temperature controller). It equals sleep, and that's priceless.

Bruce Langseth, Pigs in Peril: The Taylor countdown timer. It lets me know when it's time for things like wood chips, basting, and turning without having to look at a clock every five minutes.

Mike Wozniak, QUAU: Thermopen is something no cook should be without. It's extremely quick and accurate. The BBQ Guru is also great. It is bliss knowing that when I go to sleep for a few hours at a competition the temperature I set the Guru to will be the exact pit temperature when I wake up.

Kevin Huls and Scott Larson, Mope & Dope Smokers: Our barbecue smokers. We couldn't do what we do without them.

Gabriel Antunez, BBQ Freaks: We couldn't do without our BBQ Guru DigiQ.

Jose Bengoa, Yolanda Bolivar, BBQ Freaks, and Steve Renfro, Flyboy BBQ: My pigtail turner. It's great for moving chicken around in a smoker. It gives you good reach, and it's easy to use.

Doug Pierce, Bonnie Q: I don't go without my antique bellows. I use it to keep my coals hot!

Kelly Wertz, 4 Legs Up: What our kids call Mr. Flippy—a spatula/tong combination for turning meat. It's great because it does not poke the meat, and you can get a grip on several burgers at once or make sure you don't drop that steak!

Direct vs. Indirect Grilling

Direct grilling is a method of quickly cooking food by placing it on a grill rack directly over the heat source. It works best with smaller portions of food and foods that require short cooking times, such as burgers and well-trimmed steaks and chops. It is faster than indirect cooking because the intense heat cooks fast and browns the outside of foods. Food is often cooked uncovered on a charcoal grill but covered on a gas grill.

Indirect grilling is a method of grilling slowly, to one side of the heat source, over a drip pan, in a covered grill. It is ideal for larger cuts of meat that require longer cooking times. Hot air circulates around the food, much as it does in a convection oven. This is the style of cooking commonly referred to as "barbecuing," and most of the recipes in this book use it.

While most people insist on poking, twisting, and flipping grilled items every 15 seconds, resist the urge and limit turns to no more than two per side. Meat, fish, or poultry that normally sticks to the grates will release naturally, while the food will be able to absorb all the great color and flavor the grill has to offer.

—Clint Cantwell, Smoke in Da Eye

SOME OF OUR FAVORITE GRILLING AND SMOKING TIPS

Using lighter fluid is a very popular way to light your fire, but we agree with the BBQ Freaks of San Juan, Puerto Rico, when they advise, "Never, ever use lighter fluid. It just doesn't taste good." It adds a chemical taste to your food.

To use a chimney starter, stuff the bottom with paper, turn the chimney over, put it on the fire grate, fill it with briquettes (around ninety-two in a standard chimney), and set the paper on fire. The fire then moves to the coals, and once the coals are ash gray (20 to 30 minutes), use a fireproof glove or mitt to grasp the chimney handle and dump the hot coals on the fire grate.

A drip pan can tame the mess during indirect cooking. You can buy a disposable aluminum pan or improvise one using a sheet of heavy-duty aluminum foil about two and a half times as large as the food you will be cooking. Fold the foil in half; then fold up the edges to make 2-inch-high sides. Crease the corners to seal.

To make a water pan for smoking, place an aluminum bread pan (or larger size) in the bottom of your cooker next to the coals and fill it with water.

You can help keep your meat moist while cooking by spritzing it with apple juice, which won't change the flavor of the finished meat.

Don't be afraid to make adjustments based on your observations. If the recipe says to cook for 20 minutes a side, and the meat is getting browned after 3 minutes, lower the heat. If the meat is not starting to brown after 5 minutes, raise the heat. If you see your food is browning unevenly across the grate, move it around. Just pay attention and use all your senses. When something starts to burn, you can smell it. You can see the smoke change color. You can hear the sizzling. You can tell if the meat is done by touching it. You can also feel how hot the coals are.
—Chris Capell, Dizzy Pig

Finding ways to take tougher cuts of meat over the top is central to the art of grilling and barbecue. But despite having the perfect recipe and the perfect execution, your brisket, flank steak, or flat iron steak is still going to taste like a dry, chewy shoe if you don't slice it across the fibrous grains that run through the meat.
—Clint Cantwell, Smoke in Da Eye

Do not sauce too early; it burns easily on the fire.
—BBQ Freaks

Cleaning Your Grill Grates

It's easiest to clean your grill grates after you've used them, when they're still warm. Scrub stainless-steel grates with brass-wire brushes, and scrub cast-iron grates with stainless-steel brushes. You can also use crumpled pieces of foil to remove buildup.

Another way to clean them is to turn up your gas grill to high or build a hot fire in a charcoal grill and cover the entire grate with heavy-duty foil, weigh it down with bricks or rocks, cover the grill, and let it burn for about 10 minutes. Remove the foil with tongs and dispose of it. Hit the grate with a long-handled brush and the charred bits will turn to powder that will fall off into the fire.

Charcoal for Grilling or Smoking

You can buy two different kinds of charcoal. Charcoal briquettes made of compacted ground charcoal, coal dust, and starch are most common. They come in standard and easy-lighting. Easy-lighting briquettes are pretreated with a lighting solution for a quick start and need to burn for only 10 minutes before they are ready for grilling. They can be a real time-saver, but we don't recommend them because they can lend a petrochemical flavor to whatever you are grilling or barbecuing. You can also use lump charcoal, the carbon residue of wood that has been charred, usually in the form of lumps.

Woods for Smoking

Natural wood chips and chunks can be added to a fire to impart a smoky flavor to food as it cooks. Alder, apple, cherry, hickory, maple, mesquite, oak, and pecan are commonly used.

The chips are soaked in water for about an hour, drained well, and added to a fire just before putting food on the grill. In kettle grills or gas grills, water-soaked wood chips or dry smoke pellets work best. For charcoal cookers, just dump them on top of the hot coals or flames.

If you're using a large cooker that takes wood chunks, use seasoned wood that was split and dried for at least 6 months prior to cooking. The moisture in fresh wood creates creosote and gives the meat a bitter taste. Also use different types of wood to layer flavors on the meat. Fruitwoods go well with chicken, pork, and fish. They can also give a nice color to the meat. Pecan wood is great on brisket.

—Paul Schatte, Head Country II

For gas grills, place the soaked chips in heavy-duty foil, make a package, seal the edges, poke holes in the top, and place the package on the hot burner or lava rock. Use tongs to remove and dispose of the package afterward when cool. Large cookers with a firebox on the side take well to wood logs or chunks. Follow the manufacturer's directions.

We encourage all cooks, indoors and out, to think local and cook local. This applies to where you get your meat, your produce, your beverages, and any other essentials needed to host a backyard barbecue. That also means it is best to smoke with local hardwoods. In the Pacific Northwest, that would be alder. In Texas it's mesquite or oak—red, white, or post oak, depending on where you live in Texas. In the Northeast, maple. Hedge apple wood is used by some Kansas cooks, who say it burns as hot as mesquite. Midwesterners and many southerners also have an abundant supply of hickory, oak, apple, pecan, and other wood from fruit trees that make excellent cooking and smoking woods. Floridians have orange tree wood statewide, as well as several varieties of oak, persimmon, and other hardwoods suitable for smoking. Find out what woods are abundant and available in your area and experiment with small samples of meat to see what works best—or doesn't work at all—for you. If you're partial to a certain wood that isn't local, barbecue woods of any variety can be shipped worldwide from a variety of suppliers.

Testing Grill Temperature

Most grills have thermometers, and you can also purchase one. If you plan to do a lot of barbecuing, it's a good investment. If you don't have a grill thermometer, you need to be able to judge how hot the heat is that's coming from your grill. Hold your hand, palm down, where your food will cook and at the same height as the food that will be grilled. Count each second you can hold your hand there.

1 second (or less) = Very Hot Fire —600°F or higher

2 seconds = Hot Fire—550°–599°F

3 seconds = Medium-Hot Fire—500°–549°F

4 seconds = Medium Fire—400°–499°F

5 seconds = Low-Medium Fire—301°–399°F

6 seconds (or more) = Low Fire—300°F or less

These are rough estimates and can vary depending on where you place your hand. For example, there may be more heat in one location than another.

An easy way to modify your grill to fit a grill thermometer is to take a wine cork and drill a hole the diameter of your thermometer through the middle, from top to bottom. Fit the cork into one of the top grill vents and push the thermometer through the hole in the cork. That way you can constantly monitor the internal temperature and your thermometer won't touch the metal of the grill, which could give you an inaccurate reading.

Avoiding Flare-Ups

Sometimes meat juices drip into the coals, briquettes, or rocks, causing flare-ups that can burn your meat and wreck a great meal in seconds.

To avoid flare-ups, place the meat opposite the heat source. This creates a cool zone so that you can move meat back and forth from flames to cool zone as necessary. Trimming excess fat from the meat also helps prevent flare-ups. You can also try lowering the heat by raising the grill rack and spreading the coals so there is more space between them. Or you can remove some of the coals or cover the grill.

For excessive flare-ups in a charcoal grill, you may need to remove the meat from the grill and mist the flames with a water-spray bottle. Once the flames die down, you can return the food to the grill and resume grilling. Our friend the late Giancarlo Giannelli and many other Tuscan chefs kept a bowl of salt near the grill for tossing on excessive flare-ups.

Do not mist flare-ups on a gas grill. Simply close the lid and wait for the flare-up to die down. Some lava rock systems can collect grease that may result in flare-ups, so be especially watchful when using them and change them once a season if you use your grill a lot. When you open your propane tank valve, it might help to give it only one turn so that you can shut it off in a hurry in the event of a flare-up.

Testing for Meat Doneness

A meat thermometer guarantees perfectly cooked meat every time. Insert the meat thermometer into the center of the thickest part of the uncooked meat, not touching any fat, bone, or the grill. The chart on pages 11 and 13 gives suggested doneness temperatures for a variety of meats.

Just because your beautiful steak or pork chop is done grilling doesn't mean it's finished cooking. Due to carryover heat, internal temperatures will increase roughly 10 more degrees after being removed from the heat, meaning a medium-rare steak should be pulled at 125° to 130°F rather than the desired 135° to 140°F.

—Clint Cantwell, Smoke in Da Eye

Some pros prefer not to use a meat thermometer because, as Bill Gillespie of Smokin' Hoggz puts it, "One of the worst things you can do to a piece of meat is to start jabbing it with a probe to see if it is done. You'll let all of the juices out and end up with a dry piece of meat." Instead, Bill uses what he calls the finger test:

RAW: Open the palm of your hand. Relax the hand. Take the index finger of your other hand and push on the fleshy area between the thumb and the base of the palm. Make sure your hand is relaxed. This is what raw meat feels like.

WELL DONE: Now gently press the tip of your pinky and your thumb together. Again feel the fleshy area below the thumb. It should feel quite firm. This is what well-done meat feels like when you press on it.

MEDIUM: Press the tip of your ring finger and your thumb together. The flesh beneath the thumb should give a little more. This is what meat cooked to a medium doneness feels like.

MEDIUM-RARE: Gently press the tip of your middle finger to the tip of your thumb. This is medium rare.

RARE: Press the tip of your index finger to the tip of your thumb. The fleshy area below the thumb should give quite a bit. This is what meat cooked to rare feels like. Open up your palm again and compare raw to rare.

Chef Paul likes to go by feel too, but until you get your bearings, he suggests using a meat thermometer for safety. For a list of suggested temperatures for meat doneness, see the following chart.

After some practice, a meat thermometer becomes almost like the toothpick-in-a-cake method of checking doneness. When the thermometer probe slides easily into the hunk of meat, you get a feel for doneness. (But until you get that feel, read the temperature on the dial.) A meat hook is also helpful. It allows you to pick up and move meat easily on the smoker.

—Paul Schatte, Head Country II

Food Doneness and Temperature

	DONENESS	INTERNAL TEMPERATURE °F
BARBECUED PORK	Sliceable and Chopped	180°F (82.2°C)
SHOULDERS, PICNICS	Sliceable, Pullable, and Chopped	185°F (85° C)
BOSTON BUTTS	Pullable	195° to 205°F (91° to 96°C)
BARBECUED BEEF BRISKET	Sliceable	185°F (85°C)
BEEF STEAKS	Rare	135°F (57°C)
	Medium-Rare	140°F (60°C)
	Medium	145°F (63°C)
	Medium-Well	160°F (71°C)
	Well Done	170°F (77°C)
BEEF ROAST	Rare	130°F (54°C)
	Medium-Rare	140°F (60°C)
	Medium	145°F (63°C)
	Medium-Well	160°F (71°C)
	Well Done	170°F (77°C)
CHICKEN Whole or Pieces	Done	170°F (77°C)
Breast	Done	165°F (74°C)
CORNISH HEN	Done	170°F (77°C)
DUCK	Done	170°F (77°C)
GROUND MEAT	Medium	165°F (74°C)
BEEF, PORK, LAMB	Well Done	170°F (77°C)
HAM Fully Cooked	Well Done	140°F (60°C)
Not Fully Cooked	Well Done	160°F (71°C)
LAMB CHOPS AND RACK	Rare	120°F (49°C)
	Medium-Rare	125°F (52°C)
	Medium	130°F (54°C)
	Medium-Well	140°F (60°C)
LAMB ROAST	Rare	115°F (46°C)
	Medium-Rare	125°F (52°C)
	Medium	130°F (54°C)
	Medium-Well	140°F (60°C)
PHEASANT	Well Done	165°F (74°C)

(continued on page 13)

WHETHER YOU ARE NEW TO BARBECUING OR A SEASONED PRO, YOU ARE NOT IMMUNE TO DISASTERS. ALWAYS KEEP THIS IN MIND AND TAKE PRECAUTIONS TO AVOID PREDICTABLE DISASTERS. IT'S ALSO A GOOD IDEA TO LEARN FROM THESE BAD DAY PIT STORIES:

Early in my barbecue career, during the Christmas holidays, all my family was visiting. I loaded my Lang 84 with fifteen slabs of baby back ribs. Most of the family was upstairs watching football. My wife and three nieces were shopping. It was raining very steadily, so I had my 10- by-10 E-Z UP over the smoker. I had failed to notice that a 6-foot folding table and a plastic tote full of charcoal were sitting in the back of the trailer next to the firebox. Needless to say, when you place fuel and combustible items next to an un-insulated firebox, they will catch on fire!

The wife and girls returned and frantically honked the horn. I thought, What the heck does she want? I rushed outside in the rain to find 10-foot flames shooting up through what used to be my E-Z UP. Fortunately, the rain prevented me from setting the neighborhood on fire. But the E-Z UP, table, and the rest of the items on the trailer were history. My brother-in-law and I managed to get the fire put out without having to call the fire department. The good news was that the ribs were fine and our holiday dinner was saved. Moral of the story: always check your area before firing up your pit!
—Scott Burton, South Pork BBQ Team

I invited the entire family and neighborhood over for smoked ribs. I was experimenting with a new smoker and got the heat shot up way too high. So I shut the drafts and closed the chimney damper. "Creosote anyone?" The bones had smoke rings!
—Bruce Langseth, Pigs in Peril

As a competition cook, it's probably best never to acknowledge that there might have been a disaster at some point. Truth be told, all of us have been there, and some of the best tales around concern hotshot barbecue cooks who have had a less-than-great day.

Many years ago, a buddy and I were cooking for a party of about fifty people. We had two Weber Ranch Kettles, and on one of the grills we had a large whole halibut stuffed with herbs, good olive oil, garlic, salt, and pepper. We had fired up just one corner of the grill to cook with indirect heat.

The kitchen was close to the backyard, and we made several trips inside to attend to other parts of the meal. As the tempo picked up near mealtime, I wanted to go outside and take a last look at the progress of the halibut. We were busy, but we had control, and the last thing I was worried about was how the fish was getting along.

There were a lot of people in the backyard, and as the evening temperature had cooled down, many of them were crowding around the grills. I worked my way through the crowd, taking questions about the meal, and in general enjoying myself. I squeezed in near the grill, opened it, and was met by a wall of heat unlike anything I'd ever experienced. Apparently one of the guests had decided they didn't like all that smoke coming out of the grill's vent, and had closed it, causing the heat to build up inside. After I opened the lid, I realized something smelled funny—and it wasn't the halibut.

PORK CHOPS	Medium-Rare	130°F (54°C)
	Medium	140°F (60°C)
	Medium-Well	150°F (66°C)
PORK TENDERLOIN	Medium-Rare	135°F (57°C)
	Medium	140°F (60°C)
	Medium-Well	150°F (66°C)
SAUSAGE	Well Done	170°F (77°C)
TURKEY		
Whole	Done (Check Thigh)	175°F (79°C)
Breast	Done	165°F (74°C)
Dark Meat	Done	175°F (79°C)
VEAL CHOPS & ROAST	Medium-Rare	125°F (52°C)
	Medium	140°F (60°C)
	Medium-Well	150°F (66°C)
VENISON	Medium	160°F (71°C)

t was my now nonexistent eyelashes and parts of my eyebrows. Fortunately none of the guests were injured, and the halibut and the rest of the food turned out great, so the disaster was at least not of the gastronomic kind. Eyelashes grow back, and since then I have never failed to check my vents before lifting the lid on a grill.
—Craig Whitson of Norway

was waiting for the food editor of the *Toronto Star* to do an article on barbecue and grilling. She had interviewed me before, and we got chatting about different things. While we talked, the caramel apple pizza perfection that had so carefully prepared on the grill burned to a crisp. Luckily the top didn't show too many burn marks, so the photographer still took a picture and the article ran.
—Danielle Dimovski, Diva Q BBQ

Letting Meat Rest

When the meat reaches the desired doneness, remove it from the grill. Let it stand, covered with a tent of aluminum foil, for 10 to 15 minutes before slicing. This will allow the juices to redistribute and make the meat easier to slice.

I like to hold meat for 20 to 30 minutes in a clean, dry ice chest (without ice) to allow the moisture to be reabsorbed by the meat. The resting period also allows the meat to firm up for better slicing. Remember, your guests will eat with their eyes first. Go for appearance and the WOW factor!

—Paul Schatte, Head Country II

Backyard Barbecue Planning Checklist

As with all checklists, treat this one as a starting point to use in building your own.

If a checklist is too over the top for you, there's nothing wrong with spontaneous, unplanned events. As Diva Q told us, "The best backyard barbecues are the ones that are not planned down to the last minute—the ones that are spontaneous."

What to Do Ahead of Time

- Check the weather forecast before you set the date and invite guests. Mother Nature can be fickle, but at least you can try to better your odds of avoiding inclement weather on the day of your event.

- Prepare your invitation list and invite guests at least a week ahead, but preferably two.

- Have a backup plan for what to do if the weather turns bad on the day or evening of your event. Set up a tent for just-in-case? Dine in the garage? Dine in your house? Call the guests and tell them the venue has changed to Famous Ken's Ribs & Butts, your treat?

- Plan the menu and decide who is responsible for each item on the menu. Are you providing all the food and beverages?

- Make a list of all the food and supplies you'll need. Do this as far ahead as possible. You'll think of stuff to add as time goes on. Basic items on the list will be:

1. meat (¼ pound raw product per diner as a rule of thumb; when in doubt ask your local butcher or meat cutter)

2. plates, cups, silverware, napkins, paper towels, tablecloths

3. beverages to make or buy ahead

4. ice

5. washcloths you can wet with warm water so each guest can clean his or her hands from hands-on dining such as rib eating

- Develop a timetable. What can be made ahead of time? What has to be made the day of the event? Chart out cooking times and temperatures. Chart out serving time with a backup time and a plan to keep everyone occupied and satisfied in case of delays.

- Make a to-do list of everything you can accomplish before the guests arrive. A good host will give guests as much undivided attention as possible instead of running around doing stuff that could have been done ahead of time.

- Plan ahead for insect and varmint control. Uninvited guests such as mosquitoes and ants can put a damper on everyone's fun.

- Plan where guests will congregate when they arrive and when it's time for the main course. Will you have appetizers and beverages at a serve-yourself station, or will you and cohosts serve them? Do you expect guests to eat and run or make a day or evening of it?

- Make a welcome sign that also directs guests where to go if you're not at the front door to greet them: "Welcome! Come on in" or "Welcome! Please come in to the backyard."

Welcome backyard!

CHAPTER 2: The Kansas City Barbeque Society (KCBS) has had a lot of fun over the years with the motto "Barbecue: it's not just for breakfast anymore!" In the barbecue competition network, that motto is part tongue-in-cheek but mostly reality, especially at contests. Many contest cooks take their breakfasts seriously. Even on the morning of a competition, when they're focused on orchestrating all contest details on pace with the turn-in clock, breakfast is not overlooked. And since breakfast is not a contest category, the champs can be as creative or elaborate as they wish, though a lot of their best day-starters are surprisingly simple.

For breakfast with a Tex-Mex flair we channeled our fond memories of breakfasts in Texas and put together our own version of a Texas backyard barbecue migas recipe.

When you try Frank and Ed's Screaming Redneck Breakfast Sandwich, you'll be inspired to host a Screaming Redneck Backyard Breakfast for the whole family and maybe even some friends and neighbors. It's that good.

We recently discovered a perfect substitute term for breakfast that resonates well with the KCBS motto. When Margaret S. Fox was owner-chef of the famous Café Beaujolais in Mendocino, California, she coauthored a book of recipes with John Bear under the title *Morning Food: Café Beaujolais*. We love the concept, as well as the book, and as far as we're concerned, you can expand the "morning food" concept to any recipe in this book. After all, barbecue isn't just for lunch or dinner anymore!

Break-fast

Screaming Redneck Breakfast Sandwich

Serves 8 to 10

Eddie Tonino and Frank Kondor's ciabatta egg sandwich with country sausage, bacon, and cheese is a memorable meal any time of day or night. Just thinking about it makes us hungry! According to the guys of Redneck Caviar, there is simply no better smell on a competition morning than that of smoking meats mixed with the added essence of frying bacon and sausage. Add some eggs and cheese and, man, you have a sandwich that keeps you full until the last turn-in. They get their rolls from a Portuguese bakery. You can make the meat ahead and freeze it in an airtight container so that you're ready to assemble the sandwich in a hurry when you need to feed a crowd.

2½ pounds very lean boneless pork butt

8 ounces pork fat

1 tablespoon kosher salt

1½ teaspoons dried sage, crushed

1 teaspoon white pepper

1 teaspoon brown sugar

½ teaspoon dried thyme, crushed

¼ teaspoon dried marjoram, crushed

⅛ teaspoon ground cloves

¼ teaspoon hot red pepper flakes

Olive oil, for brushing

8 to 10 ciabatta rolls, for serving

2 tablespoons unsalted butter

12 large eggs

¼ cup water

8 to 10 slices provolone cheese

2 pounds thinly sliced bacon, cooked until crisp

8 to 10 slices cheddar cheese

Prepare a medium-hot grill.

Grind the meat and fat finely in a meat grinder. Place it in a large mixing bowl and mix in the salt, sage, pepper, brown sugar, thyme, marjoram, cloves, and hot red pepper flakes. Then finely grind again. Form the mixture into patties. Place the patties on the grill and cook for 7 to 10 minutes. Turn and cook for 7 to 10 minutes more, or until a digital thermometer inserted into the center of a patty registers 160°F.

Brush olive oil on the inside of each ciabatta roll and grill the inside only until toasted.

Melt the butter in a large nonstick skillet over medium heat. In a medium bowl, lightly whisk the eggs until combined. Whisk in the water. Pour the mixture into the skillet and cook, stirring, until the eggs are tender and fluffy.

To assemble each sandwich, stack 1 slice provolone, 1 sausage patty, a roll-size portion of the scrambled eggs, 4 slices bacon, latticed, and 1 slice cheddar cheese. Top with the other half of the roll and enjoy.

EDDIE TONINO AND FRANK KONDOR, REDNECK CAVIAR

Ed and I started down the remarkable barbecue trail about 3 years ago. After our first contest we were hooked. Like everyone else who starts this adventure, you go into your first contest thinking no one has better barbecue than you. Man, were we rudely awakened. It is 3 years later and we are still in search of the perfect combination of smoke and flavor that wins contests. We have had some success along the way and lots of head scratching with some of the results. But all that aside, man, have we had fun. Our adventures on the barbecue circuit have led us to making our own sausage and bacon, smoked in my backyard in a stone pizza oven.

Pigs in Peril Barbecue Sausage Sandwich

Serves 6 to 8

Bruce Langseth recommends this for your backyard barbecue when you're tired of the usual burgers and hot dogs. It is easy, different, and delicious. Use mild sausage instead of hot if your guests don't have a fiery tooth. Bruce credits his brother Brian for coming up with the sauce recipe. He says it adds flavor and tones down the heat.

6 ears fresh sweet corn in the husks, soaked in warm water for 1 hour

SAUSAGE MIXTURE

1 pound Jimmy Dean hot sausage

1 pound Jimmy Dean regular sausage

½ cup finely diced red bell pepper

½ cup finely diced onion

1 clove garlic, smashed beyond all recognition

Pinch of salt

1 tablespoon coarsely ground black pepper

SAUCE

2 cups packed brown sugar

2 cups ketchup

¼ cup soy sauce

¼ cup white vinegar

Hoagie buns, for serving

Preheat a smoker to 250°F.

Remove the husks from the sweet corn and set the corn aside for another use.

In a large bowl, combine both kinds of sausage, the red bell pepper, onion, garlic, salt, and black pepper and mix well. Roll the mixture into small balls, fold them into the cornhusks, and flatten them out. Place the filled husks on the smoker and cook for 1 to 1½ hours, or until the meatballs are done, using a handful of apple and hickory chips about 15 minutes into the cooking process.

Make the sauce: Place the sauce ingredients in a slow cooker set on medium. Remove the meatballs from the husks and place them in the slow cooker, making sure they are covered by the sauce. Turn the heat to low and let warm for at least 2 hours.

Place the meatballs and sauce in hoagie buns and serve.

BRUCE AND LIN LANGSETH, PIGS IN PERIL

After 3 years of judging barbecue as a Kansas City Barbeque Society–certified judge, I decided I would rather be smoking at the pit than sitting in a vinyl tent with ambient temperatures of 90 degrees for a couple of hours. It wasn't that much fun, especially since the party was going on outside!

Before I got involved in competition barbecue, I had never in my life cooked a rib, brisket, or pork butt. I had incinerated a few chickens, but the food I would toss on a plate and present to my family and friends never seemed to fire them up too much. It wasn't long before I noticed a lot of family and friends were very busy cleaning out their garages, painting fences, or polishing their goldfish when the barbecue invites went out. That was my final incentive to sharpen my cooking skills by competing in contests. Now that I'm competing, family and friends are always checking in to see what's cooking.

When you're competing, you can't stagnate! You have to keep improving. Otherwise, you are just tossing the $500 entry fee, meat, and other expenses into the garbage along with your low-scoring, underdone chicken, and rubberized brisket.

SERIOUSLY BBQ MEXICAN KUKUH

In Mexico the use of cocoa beans was all-important; they were even used as a currency. So they are well named as "the food of the gods." The by-product of this wonderful concoction is that this ingredient is really good for personal well-being and can supply the energy needed for a day of hard work. This recipe for a wholesome drink is different from your normal hot cocoa drink, and it is blended to your liking. As such, there are no weights and measures.

Take a handful of cocoa beans and toast them over a stove. Crack open the shells and remove the cacao nibs. (You could also buy cocoa nibs already out of their shells.) Grind the nibs to a smooth paste with a pestle and mortar and add a little black pepper and ground corn, making sure to maintain a pasty consistency. Moisten with warm water and add a pinch of hot red pepper flakes. The object is to not heat your mouth but to give a soothing warmth in the back of your throat. Add enough water or warm cream to fill a tall glass and sweeten to taste with palm sugar or honey. You can also add cinnamon, allspice, and/ or nutmeg if you like. Serve hot or chilled. For a shortcut: Where cocoa beans or nibs are not available, buy the best chocolate you can— at least 70% cocoa. Melt the chocolate and gently stir in water or warm cream. Continue with the recipe.

The Baron's Barbecue Bubble 'n' Squeak

Serves 8

Bubble and squeak is a traditional English/Scottish dish. Chef Paul once entered a Cajun bubble and squeak recipe in a national catfish cook off in Jackson, Mississippi, and made the mistake of assuming he should hold back on the spiciness just a little. Alas, he took fifth. He later got second place with a similar recipe in a Wolferman's contest, and he has refined it again for us here. The bubble refers to the oysters or catfish nuggets, and the squeak refers to the pig—in this case bacon and pulled pork, though sometimes he likes to use brisket.

½ medium head cabbage, sliced

8 slices bacon, diced

1 yellow onion, thinly sliced

1 cup pulled pork or cubed and chopped brisket point

1 pint fresh oysters or catfish nuggets

1 tablespoon unsalted butter

3 cups shredded hash brown potatoes, fresh, or frozen and thawed

½ teaspoon paprika

Salt and freshly ground black pepper

8 large eggs, fried to desired doneness and kept warm

In a medium saucepan over medium-high heat, cook the cabbage in a small amount of water for about 5 minutes, or until tender. Drain and set aside.

In a well-seasoned cast-iron skillet over medium heat, cook the bacon and onion until the onion is soft and the bacon is cooked. Add the pork and oysters and cook until heated through. Add the butter and then mix in the cooked cabbage and the potatoes. Season with paprika, salt, and pepper. Cook until browned on the bottom, turn, and brown again.

To serve, divide the potato mixture among 8 plates and top each with a fried egg.

JIM'S CAMP COFFEE

Bring ½ gallon of water to a boil over an open fire or camp stove. After enough fir needles have naturally fallen into the water, put a lid on it, and bring it to a boil. Then mix 1 cup of ground coffee beans with a beaten egg or two. Drop the coffee-and-egg mixture into the boiling water. The egg will cook, thereby causing the coffee to gel; this keeps the grounds together in one glob. Keep the pot on a low boil or simmer for 5 minutes or so. The coffee-egg glob can be lifted out of the pot, or just pour around it.

You can serve the coffee in tin cups, but they can get too hot to handle. Therefore, we add some Jack Daniel's whiskey or Bailey's Irish Cream to the cup, strictly for cooling purposes of course.

Remus and the Baron's Backyard Barbecue Migas

Serves 6 to 8

We've enjoyed migas so much during our travels in central Texas that we thought surely some of our Texas barbecue champions would come up with a barbecue version for this book. We asked, but we did not receive, so here's our own version. Our friend John Raven insists that true migas do not include beans. To him it is blasphemy to put beans and eggs on the same plate. On the other hand, all of the migas we've been served in Texas have included beans, pinto or black, whole or refried. We like it that way, no blasphemy intended. This one is easy, can be made indoors or out, and will please your breakfast guests morning, noon, or night. We recommend a large cast-iron skillet for cooking the tortilla strips and eggs.

¼ cup corn oil

1 dozen large eggs

⅓ cup milk

Salt and freshly ground black pepper

4 tablespoons (½ stick) unsalted butter

2 (15-ounce) cans refried beans or
   3 (15-ounce) cans pinto beans
   or black beans, heated

1 pound bacon, fried to desired
   level of crispness, or 1 pound
   leftover barbecued pulled pork

6 corn tortillas, cut into ¼-inch-wide
   strips and fried until crisp (see Note)

4 cups salsa or pico de gallo, homemade,
   or your favorite brand, for serving

6 to 8 soft corn tortillas, warmed

Place the oil in a skillet and heat it over medium-high heat on a grill or stovetop. Combine the eggs, milk, salt, and pepper in a large bowl and whisk until well blended. Pour the egg mixture into the skillet, add the butter, and scramble to the desired doneness, moist or dry. When the eggs are done, immediately transfer them to a serving bowl.

Place some of the eggs on each serving plate, topped with some beans, bacon, tortilla strips, and salsa. Serve with warm tortillas.

Note: Cooks in a hurry can use store-bought tortilla chips, crumbled.

CHAPTER 3: Whether you call them starters, appetizers, or hors d'oeuvres, they play a curious culinary role. Served with drinks as a prelude to a feast, they are meant to knock the edge off your guests' hunger pangs and jump-start their appetite for the feast ahead. We've found, however, that great starters served in meal-size quantities can easily star as the main dish. It's a matter of quantity and presentation. Do pay heed to quantity. We, and most other barbecuers we know, have eaten so many great appetizers at backyard barbecues that they put a damper on our appetite for the entrée. If you serve too much of a good appetizer, be prepared for some of your guests to be too full to enjoy the main dish!

Some starters also work as snack food when your gang gathers in the backyard with a big-screen TV set up to watch movies, sports, the Oscars, or food shows. Redneck Caviar is a perfect snack for such occasions, but as great as it is, don't stop with caviar. Judging by the number of shrimp starter recipes we received, shrimp is the most popular starter among champs. We have coconut shrimp, rosemary shrimp, cheesy bacon jalapeño shrimp, and honey mustard shrimp. We even have our own original explanation of why shrimp is so popular among landlocked Oklahoma barbecue champions.

For your guests who avoid seafood, we have Dizzy Pig's fantastic Tsunami Duck Breast, Jeff Brinker's Fried Rice Balls, plus stuffed mushrooms from the Beaver Castors, stuffed jalapeños from Jeff Brown, and a wake-up-call fiery and frosty chicken salad from Madison's legendary pitmaster, Smoky Jon Olson. Many of our main dishes can be reduced to starter size as well. Because these starters are so delicious, it bears repeating: serve small quantities. Leave your guests hungry for the main course.

Starters

Beaver Castors Stuffed Grilled Mushrooms

Serves 6 to 8

Jim Erickson of the Beaver Castors (see page 121) says he uses these as a starter when grilling steaks. If you want to stretch the recipe a bit, finely chop some of the mushroom stems and cook them in with the sausage, garlic, and scallion. Jim sautés the mushroom stems in butter and garlic for a steak topping.

Jim used to use bear sausage, but this recipe works great with any sage breakfast sausage such as Jimmy Dean, or even a sweet Italian-style sausage. You can even start with a cased link sausage and remove the sausage from the casings before mixing.

This can be prepared ahead of time if kept refrigerated; doing this makes for quick hors d' oeuvres when guests arrive.

1 pound bulk sausage

1 scallion, white and green parts, minced

1 large clove garlic, minced

½ cup panko breadcrumbs

1 (8-ounce) package cream cheese, softened

2 tablespoons finely chopped fresh parsley

⅓ cup freshly grated Parmesan cheese

1 teaspoon MSG (optional)

¼ teaspoon cayenne

24 large fresh white button or cremini mushrooms, stems removed

Dry white wine, for brushing

Prepare a medium-hot grill for direct grilling.

Cook the sausage, scallion, and garlic in a large skillet over medium-high heat, stirring frequently, until the sausage is cooked, 10 to 12 minutes; drain. Return the sausage to the skillet and add the panko, cream cheese, parsley, Parmesan, MSG, if using, and cayenne. Mix well and cook over low heat until the cream cheese becomes very soft.

Before you stuff the mushrooms, you may want to use a teaspoon to carefully expand the cavities. Place the mushroom caps cavity side up on a tray and brush with the dry white wine. Stuff the mushrooms with the filling, mounding it slightly. Transfer the mushrooms from the tray to the grill grate, but don't place them directly over the coals. Cover the grill and cook until the mushrooms become tender, 20 to 25 minutes. Remove from the grill and let cool for a few minutes before serving.

Wildcatters Stuffed Jalapeños

Serves 6 to 8

Oilfield jargon pegs wildcatters as speculators who take a chance on drilling for oil in areas where there is no guarantee of finding it. When oil detection was high on intuition and low on technology, wildcatters drilled more dry holes than gushers. Wildcatting still involves speculation and determination—a true wildcatter never gives up. They keep trying until, as in *Giant* and other movies, "black gold" is struck and the crew is delirious with joy. Jeff Brown is a true wildcatter. Based in Enid, Oklahoma, Jeff and his Wildcatters Q Crew Competition BBQ Team is one of the winningest teams in the circuit. Jeff cooks the way he wildcats. He keeps trying until he gets it right. Try this Wildcatters Q version of a classic favorite starter and you'll agree that Jeff struck gold with this one!

8 ounces garden vegetable cream cheese, at room temperature

8 ounces onion and chive cream cheese, at room temperature

1 cup real bacon bits

1 teaspoon Greek seasoning or seasoning of your choice

20 jalapeños, cored and seeded

1 pound thinly sliced bacon

Prepare a medium-hot grill.

In a medium bowl, combine the cream cheeses and blend until smooth. Add the bacon bits and Greek seasoning and mix well.

Using an icing gun or a zipper bag with a corner cut off, stuff the jalapeños with the cream cheese mixture. Place one end of a slice of bacon over the open part of the jalapeño, wrap the bacon around the entire jalapeño, and use a toothpick or skewer to secure it. Place the jalapeños on the grill, cover, and cook for about 15 minutes before turning and cook for 15 to 20 minutes more, or until the bacon is done.

JEFF BROWN, WILDCATTERS

I'm head cook of the Wildcatters Q Crew, which also includes Tracy Brown (wife), Little Izzy (daughter), Anna Brown (mom), and Henry Brown (dad). I became involved in competition barbecuing in 2005 when Enid, Oklahoma, had its first competition. We were vendors selling pellet grills and thought we would try competing. My first brisket was tough as a baseball mitt, and my chicken was not finger lickin'. The year 2006 was better, and in 2007 we received our first first-place call in ribs and were hooked. Barbecuing is something the whole family enjoys. Last year alone we competed in thirty-four competitions.

Paul Schatte's Head Country II Shrimp on Rosemary Skewers

Serves 4 to 6

When we were putting together this book, our editor asked us, "Why so many shrimp recipes from Oklahoma?" Given that Oklahoma is landlocked, far from any ocean, we were baffled too. After dismissing the idea that being landlocked makes Oklahomans crave shrimp, we settled on a better explanation. Shrimp and catfish, especially the spoonbill catfish, are popular in Oklahoma today because Oklahomans subconsciously channel their primal memories back 400 million years to a time when their land was covered with a shallow prehistoric ocean where shrimp and spoonbills thrived. Our editor still hasn't bought it, but it makes sense to us!

When you and your guests take a first bite of Paul's shrimp, loaded with the flavors of butter, barbecue seasonings, lime, a hint of rosemary, and the magic of charcoal grilling, you won't care about our theory. You'll just be hoping there's plenty of shrimp for everyone.

10 sprigs fresh rosemary

2 pounds (about 40) uncooked large shrimp, peeled and deveined

8 tablespoons (1 stick) unsalted butter, melted

2 teaspoons Head Country All Purpose Championship Seasoning or your favorite seasoning

¼ cup Head Country Premium Marinade or your favorite marinade

1 lime

Prepare a medium-hot hardwood charcoal fire for direct grilling.

Remove the rosemary leaves from three-quarters of each sprig. Reserve the leaves. Place the sprigs in a bowl of water to soak for 15 minutes. Skewer 4 shrimp onto each sprig.

In a small bowl, combine the melted butter, the seasoning, marinade, and 1 tablespoon of the reserved rosemary leaves. Wrap a small strip of aluminum foil around the rosemary leaves left on the sprigs to keep the leaves from burning.

Place a layer of aluminum foil across the grill grate. Place the shrimp skewers on the foil and cook until the shrimp are drawn up and orange in color, about 5 minutes, turning 2 to 3 times and brushing with the butter mixture each time while cooking. Right before you turn the shrimp the last time, throw the remaining rosemary leaves directly over the hot coals and cover the grill to allow the smoke from the rosemary leaves to penetrate the shrimp.

Place the shrimp skewers on a platter. Remove the foil, cut the lime in half, and squeeze the lime juice over the shrimp skewers. Serve immediately.

PAUL SCHATTE, HEAD COUNTRY II

I got involved in competition barbecuing because of my dad, Ed Schatte, a championship barbecuer in his own right. He and I competed in the first annual competition in Ponca City, Oklahoma, in 1990. In 1991, Danny Head, president of Head Country Food Products, asked me to join the Head Country team. God has blessed me with winning numerous competitions, including the Jack Daniel's World Championship in 1994. I have taught classes, given seminars, and even traveled internationally teaching barbecue techniques. My barbecue story continues today, and I love it! My desire is to help every backyard chef become successful and have as much fun as I am.

Seriously BBQ's Mind-Clearing Bloody Mary Granita

Serves 4

Chef Jeremy Fowler shared a number of recipes with us, including this simple frozen and blended accompaniment to barbecue. It is not as smooth as a sorbet; instead, it has a refreshing granular texture. Try it with Seriously BBQ Sea Bass with Asparagus and Coriander, Lime, and Chili Pesto (page 123).

¾ cup superfine sugar

⅓ cup water

5 cups tomato juice or puree

6 tablespoons vodka

Juice of 2 limes

1½ tablespoons Tabasco sauce

Place the sugar and water in a small saucepan over medium heat and simmer until syrupy.

Stir in the tomato juice, vodka, lime juice, and Tabasco sauce and pour the mixture into a shallow freezer-safe container. Freeze until crystals form, then remove from the freezer and stir. Repeat the process every few hours until the mixture ices up enough to scoop.

JEREMY FOWLER, SERIOUSLY BBQ

My father wanted better things for his only son following an education in one of the oldest and best public schools in England, but he was quietly disappointed when I persuaded my mother to sign me up for four years of indentured apprenticeship to the largest and best hotel in my home town of Harrogate, North Yorkshire. It took some 12 years to gain any real foothold in the profession, and I think my dad is now rather proud of the antics I had been having around the world.

The recipes I sent are from my personal, handwritten recipe book. I call it my "penicillin book," due to the very many years I have

had it and the number of food stains that are plastered all over its pages. It serves me well as it is full of recipes reworked from ideas gleaned through hard work and much perspiration. I have over the years made many annotations and alterations with numerous drawings that motivate me when I need it. I chose the recipes for their simplicity and ease of use in my own home. Many of them appear at my "al fresco" spreads during the summer or as a treat for guests. Sadly, my family is rather unadventurous in the taste department. I put it down to God keeping me humble, as they are my worst critics.

Donny Teel's Grilled Cheesy Bacon Jalapeño Shrimp

Serves 8

Everyone in the barbecue contest network knows that when Buffalo's BBQ is competing, Donny Teel will be making several trips to the awards stage at the end of the contest. Everyone also knows that no matter how much he is urged to "Smile, Donny!" as he accepts his awards, he will never crack a smile. We haven't actually seen it, but we've heard tell that Donny can't resist a smile when he takes his first bite of these grilled shrimp! He told us it's a "favorite that we make quite often here in Sperry, Oklahoma."

A pound of bacon has about 16 slices, so that's why Donny uses 16 shrimp. You can buy U-8 shrimp, which has around 8 in a pound. Thinner bacon adheres to the shrimp better than thick bacon does. Sometimes three-quarters of a strip of bacon is about right instead of a whole strip.

16 uncooked jumbo shrimp, peeled and deveined

Olive oil, for brushing

Your favorite shrimp seasoning (Donny uses Head Country)

2 jalapeños, cored, seeded, and sliced into thin strips about three-quarters of the length of the shrimp

16 long, narrow strips of Longhorn cheese

¾ pound thinly sliced bacon

Prepare a medium-hot grill for indirect cooking.

Lightly brush the shrimp with olive oil and season it to your liking. Place a strip of jalapeño and a strip of cheese on each, then wrap with a slice of bacon, using a toothpick to secure it.

Place the shrimp on the grill over indirect heat (the bacon will cause flare-ups if placed over the heat) and cook until the bacon is done, 5 to 7 minutes per side.

DONNY TEEL, BUFFALO'S BBQ

My wife, Cindy, and I had some friends that did competitions that started in the late 1980s, so we got curious about it and did our first contest in late 1996. We have been actively competing ever since, doing as many as thirty-eight competitions in a single year.

I won Grand Champion at the Jack Daniel's World Championship Invitational Barbecue in 2005 with my Boys from Tornado Alley team. We're still winning awards under our new team name, Buffalo's BBQ, and I've branched out into owning and operating a successful barbecue business under the same name.

Que's Your Daddy Honey Mustard Shrimp

Serves 4 to 6

Although Que's Your Daddy's Doc Richardson grew up in the hills of Tennessee, his barbecue expertise stretches far beyond Tennessee's favorite ribs, whole hog, and pork shoulder. His Honey Mustard Shrimp exemplifies the adage that simple can be better. This marriage of shrimp, mustard, bacon, and butter, fresh from the grill, "has few ingredients but is big on flavor!" Doc said it. We tried it, and we believe it.

1½ pounds (24 to 30) uncooked large shrimp, peeled and deveined

1 (12-ounce) jar honey mustard

1 pound hickory-smoked bacon (not thick-cut)

Melted butter, for serving

Place the shrimp in a medium bowl. Add the honey mustard and mix well to coat evenly. Cover and refrigerate for 2 to 4 hours.

Prepare a medium-hot grill for direct grilling. If you're using wooden skewers, soak them in water.

Cut off one-third of the end of each bacon strip and reserve for another use. Wrap a shrimp with 1 piece of bacon and run a skewer through the 2 ends of the shrimp (see Note). Place another bacon-wrapped shrimp on the same skewer and repeat until there are 4 to 5 shrimp on each of the skewers.

Place the skewers on the grill over the cool zone (so the bacon doesn't burn), close the lid, and cook for about 7 minutes. Turn, close the lid, and cook for 7 minutes more, or until the bacon is crisp. Remove the skewers from the grill, baste with melted butter, and serve.

Note: The skewer should go through each shrimp twice. This prevents the shrimp from spinning on the skewer as you are turning during cooking. It also helps to hold the bacon in place.

DOC AND SUSAN RICHARDSON, QUE'S YOUR DADDY

Doc Richardson began to develop a passion for barbecue when he was young, watching his dad cook down in the hills of Tennessee. The passion grew over the next 20-plus years, and in his search for more information he found the barbecue forums. One person Doc met on a forum is Aaron Moore, fellow cook and competitor on the Big O' Dang O' BBQ team. When Aaron found out that Doc had not competed, he coaxed Doc into entering a local rib cook-off, and Que's Your Daddy BBQ team was born. Entering that competition was the worst thing that could have happened . . . Doc won his first contest that day! After the shock wore off, it was obvious that the Richardson household would never be the same. Originally the team consisted of the entire family, but it has evolved to include only Doc and his wife, Susan. They are still on speaking terms with Aaron. If it weren't for him, they never would have had the opportunity to experience the sweetness of a call or the overwhelming camaraderie of the barbecue community. Thanks, Aaron!

Jeff Brinker's Fried Rice Balls

Serves 6 to 8

Meatball possibilities are endless. First, there's your choice of ground meat—beef, veal, pork, lamb, bison, turkey, chicken, or venison, to name the most popular. Next there's a choice of what else to mix in, including seasonings. Do you follow Charlie's example on page 87, and mess around in the kitchen and come up with something different, or do you start with a standard recipe and go from there? When rice is added, they are called "porcupine balls." Jeff Brinker of B&B BBQ (see page 84) calls these "porcupine balls" with a distinctly Asian flavor profile simply, "Fried Rice Balls." We call them delicious!

DIPPING SAUCE

1 cup ketchup

¼ cup honey

¼ cup rice wine vinegar

½ cup packed brown sugar

1 teaspoon sriracha sauce

RICE BALLS

2 pounds ground boneless chicken thighs

2 cups cooked white or brown rice

¼ cup panko breadcrumbs,
   plus ¾ cup for rolling

¼ cup sugar

1 medium carrot, finely grated

2 tablespoons minced onion

1 large clove garlic, minced

¼ cup rice wine vinegar

¼ cup soy sauce

2 large eggs

½ teaspoon five-spice powder

About 2 quarts vegetable or
   peanut oil, for deep-frying

EGG WASH

2 large eggs

2 cups milk

Make the dipping sauce: Combine all the ingredients in a medium bowl and whisk until well mixed. Pour into small individual ramekins for each guest. Set aside.

Make the rice balls: Mix all the ingredients well in a large bowl. Cover and refrigerate for 2 hours.

Heat the oil in a deep cast-iron skillet or a deep-fryer to 360°F.

Form the rice mixture into balls and set them on wax paper. In a small bowl, combine the eggs and milk to make an egg wash. Dip each rice ball into the egg wash, then roll in the remaining ¾ cup of panko to coat and return them to the wax paper.

Drop the rice balls into the hot oil and cook until they float and are browned all over, 3 to 5 minutes. Strain and transfer to a paper towel–lined plate to rest for a few minutes before serving.

Burnin' Bob's Butts N Bones Coconut Shrimp

Serves 6 to 8

Although Bob and Donna Oldfield (see page 135) are famous for their beans and pork butts, they have also mastered the art of cooking brisket, chicken, ribs, and—as you'll see when you fix this recipe—shrimp. This award-winning coconut shrimp is great for an appetizer or a full dinner.

DIPPING SAUCE

1½ cups nonalcoholic piña colada mix

⅓ cup water

3 tablespoons drained canned crushed pineapple

2 tablespoons sweetened flaked coconut

3½ tablespoons confectioners' sugar

2½ teaspoons cornstarch

4 teaspoons water

SHRIMP

3 cups all-purpose flour

6 tablespoons granulated sugar

¾ teaspoon salt

½ teaspoon cayenne

3 cups whole milk

6 tablespoons Captain Morgan rum (optional, but good)

3 cups panko breadcrumbs

2½ cups sweetened flaked coconut

2 quarts peanut or canola oil

About 2½ pounds (about 40) uncooked large shrimp, peeled and butterflied, tails left on

Make the dipping sauce: Combine all of the ingredients except the cornstarch and water in a medium saucepan over medium-high heat. Simmer for 12 to 14 minutes, stirring frequently. In a small bowl, mix the cornstarch and water; slowly add it to the sauce and blend well. Continue to simmer for 5 minutes, stirring constantly. Set aside at room temperature while you make the shrimp.

Make the shrimp: Place 1 cup of the flour in a medium bowl and set aside.

In a second medium bowl, combine the remaining 2 cups of flour with the sugar, salt, cayenne, milk, and rum, if using.

In a third medium bowl, combine the panko and coconut.

In a deep cast-iron skillet or deep-fryer, heat the oil to 340°F.

While the oil is heating, dredge each shrimp in the flour and shake off the excess. Then dredge in the batter, again letting the excess drip off. Roll in the coconut mixture, coating inside the butterfly cut as well as outside. Place all the coated shrimp on a sheet of wax paper and allow the coating to set, about 10 minutes.

Fry the coated shrimp in the hot oil for 4 minutes, or until golden brown. They will float when done. Drain and cover with paper towels to remove excess oil.

Serve with the dipping sauce.

Kelly's Meatballs

Makes 52 (2-ounce) meatballs

Based on the number of recipes we received, meatballs are second only to shrimp in popularity when the barbecue champs fire up their backyard grills. This recipe from Kelly Wertz of 4 Legs Up BBQ (page 45) is so inventive and packed with spicy Mexican accents that we had to share it with you. You can plate the balls with toothpicks as a starter or try them as a main dish on pasta or tostadas.

1 (6-ounce) package corn bread stuffing mix

3 pounds ground beef

2 pounds bulk sausage

1 (28-ounce) can green enchilada sauce

1 (7.25-ounce) can Mexican-style tomato sauce

2 tablespoons hamburger or steak seasoning

1 tablespoon minced garlic

2 large eggs

1 large yellow onion, diced

3 cups shredded cheddar cheese

Preheat a grill to 350°F.

Place the stuffing mix and the contents of its seasoning packet in a food processor and process until it has the consistency of breadcrumbs.

Place the beef, sausage, enchilada and tomato sauces, seasoning, garlic, eggs, and onion in a large bowl. Mix well, but do not overmix. You don't want your meatballs to be too tightly packed. Add the shredded cheese and mix just until incorporated.

Scoop the mixture and form balls 1½ to 2 inches in diameter. Lightly oil the grill grate and place the meatballs on it. Cook for 30 to 45 minutes, or until the internal temperature of the meatballs reaches 165°F on a meat thermometer. Remove from the grill, let rest for 10 to 15 minutes, and serve. Freeze extras for quick meals later.

Abiquiu Smoked Chicken Sausages in Cornhusks

Serves 4 to 6

We don't know where Bob Palmgren, head pitmaster and proprietor of RJ's Bob-Be-Que in Mission, Kansas, got the idea for smoked sausage in cornhusks, but we credit him for inspiring our own version. Bob features a pork sausage with chopped jalapeño peppers and other seasonings. Ours pays homage to the artist Georgia O'Keeffe, who spent much of her creative life in northern New Mexico at a place called Abiquiu, taking inspiration from the local terrain. This one features a chicken sausage with chopped fire-roasted Hatch chile peppers and other New Mexico seasonings.

2 teaspoons sea salt

½ teaspoon New Mexico red chile powder, such as Rancho de Chimayo or your favorite brand

¼ teaspoon New Mexico green chile powder, such as Rancho de Chimayo or your favorite brand

1 tablespoon freshly ground black pepper

3 pounds ground chicken, turkey, pork, or beef

⅓ cup cream-style corn

2 tablespoons chopped sweet onion

2 large cloves garlic, minced

¼ cup fire-roasted Hatch chile peppers, mild or hot

2 tablespoons New Mexico honey

16 dry cornhusks, soaked in warm water for 20 minutes

16 (5-inch-long) pieces of twine

Pico de gallo or salsa, for serving

8-inch soft corn or flour tortillas, for serving

Mix the sea salt, chile powders, and black pepper together in a large bowl. Add the ground chicken, corn, onion, garlic, Hatch peppers, and honey and combine with your hands until the meat is evenly seasoned.

Remove the cornhusks from the water and place them on a cotton towel to absorb excess water.

Heat your grill or smoker to 250°F.

Form a sausage cylinder with your hands, using about 6 ounces of the sausage mixture. Set the sausage aside on a plate and repeat until you have 8 sausages. Place each sausage on a wet cornhusk, top with a second cornhusk, wrap the cornhusks around the sausage, and tie each end with twine.

Smoke for 1½ to 2 hours, or until done.

Serve with homemade pico de gallo or your favorite salsa and a soft corn or flour tortilla. You can eat them as a wrap or tostada style with a fork.

Burt's Pulled Barbecue Duck Sliders

Makes 12 sliders

Burt Culver, a fifth-generation duck farmer and barbecue aficionado, gave us this recipe that he says is "the absolute best pulled barbecue duck." Having met Burt on the competition barbecue circuit years ago and sampled his barbecue, we know this will be a winner in everyone's backyard. We like to serve this as a southern-style sandwich with some slaw on top of the pulled duck.

¼ cup Culver Competition Barbeque Rub or your favorite rub

2½ pounds duck legs or halves

12 ounces of your favorite barbecue sauce

12 slider or potato buns

Heat your smoker to 325°F.

Apply the rub to the duck meat, covering the entire surface. Place the meat on the smoker and cook until the fat is completely rendered (gone). Transfer to a plate and let sit, covered loosely with a piece of aluminum foil, for 15 minutes.

Pull the meat from the bones, chop the skin into small pieces, and mix it with the pulled meat and barbecue sauce. Serve immediately on potato buns.

BURT CULVER, THE DUCK STOPS HERE

Burt Culver is a fifth-generation duck farmer in the northern rolling hills in the Amish country of Indiana. The Culver family was the first Long Island Duck farming family, since 1858. The Culvers moved to Indiana in 1959 and now produce more than 5 million white Pekin ducks annually for the food industry.

Culver Duck (www.culverduck.com) entered the Kansas City Barbeque Society (KCBS) family in the 1990s and competed in state championships, promoting and selling barbecue duck as vendors producing their own barbecue sauce (1st place, KCBS-sanctioned Tennessee state barbecue championship) and rub (2nd place, National Barbecue Association National Competition). Culver Duck then began competing at the National Association for the Specialty Food Trade (NASFT) Fancy Food Show, winning 1 Gold and 8 Silver awards with marinated breasts, fully cooked sausage, cooked halves, and our product line.

Burnt Finger BBQ Sweet Bourbon Slush

Makes 12 to 18 drinks (depending on glass size)

This taste of the South is perfect for backyard barbecue bashes or any occasion. Megan Day of Burnt Finger BBQ keeps a bucket of Bourbon Slushes in the freezer all summer long. When company arrives, she's ready to party!

1½ cups sugar

2 cups strong hot tea (brewed with 4 large tea bags)

1 (16-ounce) can frozen orange juice concentrate

1 (12-ounce) can frozen lemonade concentrate

2½ cups bourbon, plus more for garnish

6 cups water

Orange wedges or maraschino cherries, for serving

Dissolve the sugar in the hot tea. Pour the sweetened tea, orange juice and lemonade concentrates, bourbon, and water into a large, wide freezer-safe container. Place the container, level, in the freezer. If possible, stir after 5 hours. This is not an essential step, but it helps to ensure the liquids stay mixed together. Freeze for at least 15 hours longer before serving. The consistency should be frozen but not solid.

To serve, scrape a spoon or fork over the top of the frozen mixture and scoop into a glass. Garnish with an extra splash of bourbon and an orange wedge or maraschino cherry.

JASON AND MEGAN DAY, BURNT FINGER BBQ

I wanted to get involved with competition barbecue primarily to see if I could do it. I've always loved barbecue, and the competitions circuit seemed like the next logical step from cooking in the backyard for friends and family. I also happen to be extremely competitive (and a bit of a perfectionist), so it's turned out to be the perfect creative outlet for me.

Burnt Finger BBQ Bourbon Brie

Serves 10 to 12

What better sweet treat for your party guests than brown sugar baked with bourbon and Brie? It's a flavor combination they won't forget.

1 (13- to 16-ounce) Brie cheese wheel

1½ cups packed brown sugar

1 cup bourbon

1 cup chopped walnuts

Crackers, toast, or apple slices, for serving

Prepare a medium-hot grill.

Cut the white rind off the top of the Brie wheel and place it in a pie tin. In a small bowl, combine the brown sugar and bourbon. Pour the mixture over the Brie. Top the glazed Brie with a single layer of chopped walnuts and sprinkle any extra around the sides.

Place the pie tin on the grill over indirect heat and cook for approximately 20 minutes, or until the Brie has softened and the sauce is bubbly.

Serve immediately with crackers, toast, or apple slices for dipping.

Jason Day's Fantasy Barbecue

If I could have a fantasy barbecue, the only person I would invite is my Grandpa E.J. He passed away before I started competing, but I know he would have been the number-one fan of Burnt Finger BBQ. He was a foodie in his own right, and some of my favorite childhood memories are from taking road trips with him. I used to ride along when he'd visit his sister in southern Missouri, and we'd always stop off at the Osceola Cheese Factory to sample every cheese available. For those not familiar with this glorious dairy sanctuary, it's a small cheese factory along Highway 13 in southwestern Missouri. They make close to 200 different varieties of cheese and offer up samples of damn near all of them. We'd start at the end of the cheese case and step through each and every sample cup by stabbing a bite-sized piece of cheese with a toothpick. We'd even skip lunch to save room for all the cheese samples. I know my grandpa would be extremely proud of all my barbecue accomplishments, and I'd love to share one last plate of ribs with him.

Seriously BBQ Camembert and Calvados with Rosemary

Serves 6 to 8

Chef Jeremy Fowler gave us this easy, delicious starter that will have your friends thinking you're a gourmet chef as well as a great pitmaster. Tell them to save room for the barbecue!

1 (250-gram) wheel Camembert, Le Chatelain or another brand packed in a wooden box

½ cup Calvados apple brandy

1 sprig fresh rosemary

1 cup sliced fresh figs

1 cup seedless grapes, white or red

8 to 10 breadsticks, crackers, or pretzels (Jeremy uses rosemary-flavored breadsticks)

Heat a grill or oven to 375°F (190°C if you're British, like Chef Fowler). If using a grill, heat only one side for indirect cooking.

Remove the lid from the box and cut out a cone-shaped lump of cheese from the center of the cheese (reserve it for another use). Fill the cavity with Calvados and a sprig of rosemary.

Place the cheese on the grill opposite the flames, or in the oven, close the lid or door, and cook for 25 minutes, or until soft and runny. Serve with fresh figs, juicy grapes, and breadsticks, crackers, or pretzels for dipping.

My best barbecue was while working in the Far East. I was tired and hungry, walking down a road full of hawker stalls, when a little boy jumped out and offered to cook for me. He took me to a doorway where he had a biscuit tin filled with charcoal and a grid on top. From a little chiller box, he produced some squid and set it to sizzle while I sat on a tiny stool on the pavement. One little dish appeared after another–interspersed by his running off to get me a beer, which was surprisingly chilled. The meal was delightful, a true moment in time, and thoroughly enjoyed.
—Jeremy Ravenshaw Fowler, Seriously BBQ

Redneck Caviar

Serves 8 to 10

When we met Frank Kondor and Ed Tonino (see page 19) of Milford, Connecticut, at the Mainely Grillin' & Chillin' Maine State Championship BBQ in Elliot, Maine, we asked, "Is Redneck Caviar just your team name, or do you actually make caviar?" They replied, "Stop back later and we'll treat you to our caviar and a cold beer." We did, and they did. Frank handed us each a bowl of caviar as Ed handed us a bowl of Tostitos Scoops and a cold beer. Our necks glowed red with pleasure at first bite as we suddenly felt transported to Redneck Heaven. Yes, Redneck Heaven is for real, and here's your ticket to ride!

2 (15-ounce) cans black beans, drained

2 (15-ounce) cans shoepeg corn, drained

2 (10-ounce) cans Ro-Tel tomatoes and chiles (your favorite style), drained

1 large green bell pepper, cored, seeded, and chopped

12 scallions, chopped

3 ripe tomatoes, chopped

1 jalapeño pepper, cored, seeded, and chopped

1 teaspoon garlic salt

1 teaspoon garlic powder

1 teaspoon dried parsley flakes, crushed

1 (16-ounce) bottle Italian dressing

1 (10-ounce) bag Tostitos Scoops

Place all the ingredients except the chips in a large bowl. Mix well. Serve with the chips for dipping.

Sully's Damn Dip

Serves 20

Hats off to Mike "Sully" Sullivan, Lunchmeat's right arm, Beverage Director, and notorious for his perfect BBQ Call: "BAAAHHHH-BE-QUUUUEE!!!" immortalized forever on YouTube.

Sully's Damn Dip is chips down the most famous, most sought after, get-your-chips-in-where-you-may dip in the world of barbecue competition and backyard barbecues. Be advised that this original version is not for the faint of fiery palate. At first bite you'll say either "Damn! That's good!" or "Damn! Call 911. My mouth is on fire!" Teammate Michelle Taft said it so well that we'll quote her verbatim: "This is a layered dip. Please feel free to use homemade chili, hot sauces, and/or salsas whenever possible. Make it your own, but call it The Best Damn Dip you ever had! A couple of rules come with the recipe: NO STIRRING! (This means you, Big Creek BBQ!) NO SPOONS OR BOWLS! This is a community dish. Get in there and get cozy with your neighbors! This is meant to enhance the camaraderie of teams and forms lasting friendships within the BBQ community." Believe us: Sully's Damn Dip is so good that you won't care if there are double dippers in the community!

2 (15-ounce) cans Hormel
   Hot Chili, no beans

Dirty Dick's Hot Pepper Sauce
   (aka Dirty Dick's Oral Abuse)
   or your favorite hot sauce

2 (8-ounce) packages cream cheese

½ (12-ounce) jar Dr. Gonzo's World
   Famous Peppermash (Lunchmeat likes
   the Jalapeñomash or the Supermash)

½ (16-ounce) jar Mrs. Renfro's Green Salsa

½ (16-ounce) jar Newman's Own Hot Salsa

1 (8-ounce) jar of your favorite fruity salsa

1 (8-ounce) package shredded
   mozzarella/provolone blend

Sliced jalapeños, for garnish (optional)

Tortilla chips, for serving

Prepare a medium grill.

Spread the chili on the bottom of a 17-inch cast-iron skillet. (Sully uses a paella pan.) Sprinkle some Dirty Dick's Oral Abuse over the layer of chili. Break up the cream cheese into bite-sized pieces and spread them evenly over the top. Spread the Dr. Gonzo's Peppermash over that. Spread all 3 salsas over that. Cover with the shredded mozzarella and provolone mix and garnish with jalapeños if desired.

Place the pan on the grill over the cool zone, close the lid, and cook for about 30 minutes, rotating frequently for even heating, until the whole Damn Dip is bubbling and reminds you of lava.

Serve with lots of tortilla chips.

MIKE "SULLY" SULLIVAN, LUNCHMEAT BBQ

Our team was formed by me and Gary Taft. We joined the New England Barbecue Society's Mentoring Program and were matched with Garry Howard's Smoke Ring, so we learned the ropes from a true competitor for the entire 2003 season. We then decided to jump into the proverbial fire with our own team. We persuaded our wives, Michelle and Terri, to join us, and Lunchmeat competed for the first time at the Snowshoe Grilling Challenge in 2004. At the end of that season, we ended up third overall in the NEBS Team of the Year (ToY) standings. We matched that accomplishment in 2005 and took home the coveted NEBS ToY Trophy for ribs as well. In a rare feat, we three-peated as Grand Champions at Oinktoberfest in Clarence, New York, in 2006, 2007, and 2008. We have also taken home Grands in New York, Vermont, and Pennsylvania state championships and earned Reserve Grands at numerous Massachusetts and Connecticut championships. We also won second place for brisket and placed fifth overall at the 2008 Jack Daniel's World Championship. When we're not competing, we participate in the New England Barbecue Society's many charitable endeavors, and we volunteer for cooking and judging classes as well, because we're very aware that our successes are largely due to the fact that someone took the time to mentor us. (Thanks, Garry!)

4 Legs Up Reuben Dip

Makes 2½ to 3 cups

You can serve this in one big bowl or divide it into six or seven individual ½-cup servings to avoid crowds around the bowl and allow guests to double-dip. When Reuben sandwich aficionados—and there are many, present company included—get hold of this recipe, the traditional ubiquitous French dip could take a back seat. We've tried it, and all we can say is "Wow!"

8 ounces deli corned beef, coarsely chopped

1 cup well-drained, coarsely chopped sauerkraut

1 (8-ounce) package cream cheese, softened

2 cups shredded Swiss cheese

½ cup Thousand Island dressing

Rye bread, for serving

Heat a grill to 350°F.

Mix all the ingredients except the bread in a large bowl. Pour the dip into a 9-inch square foil pan. Place on the grill, close the lid, and cook for 45 to 60 minutes, or until the mixture is bubbly and the cheese has melted through. Alternatively, you can heat in a slow cooker on low for 3 to 4 hours.

Serve with party rye bread slices or a loaf of rye bread torn into bite-sized chunks.

We catered an All Church Dinner for a country Catholic Church one Sunday noon. We got there on time, and I fired up the smoker with a brand-new load of hickory. Got it up to temp and put on the baked potatoes and smoked pork chops, then went inside to help get the serving area set up. When I came back out to check the smoker, black smoke was rolling out and the hickory—which I now know was green and wet—was just smoldering. I kicked on the propane burner, and we struggled to get back to temp. We finally got everything cooked, but of course the black creosote was all over the potatoes and pork chops. We were wiping off the black soot from the potatoes and pork chops as we served, telling the guests that this was our new Cajun Blackened recipe. Well, they loved it and came back for seconds, smiling with black teeth!
—4 Legs Up BBQ

KELLY AND RONI WERTZ, 4 LEGS UP BBQ

Our life in competition barbecue started in 2003. I, Kelly, had just finished building a second smoker and had been using it for a few weeks when I saw an ad for a KCBS contest in Omaha, Nebraska. We decided to take the kids and see what barbecue contests were all about. There was no sense in driving 300 miles without a smoker behind us, so we signed up. We still remember trying to get six full spareribs in that box for turn-ins that Saturday! We didn't get a call and finished in the middle of the pack, but we met a lot of great people and have been hooked ever since.

From that humble beginning we started catering barbecue and then opened our first restaurant in an old gas station.

South Pork New York Strip Appetizers

Serves 10 to 12

Scott often makes this appetizer the night before or the day of the barbecue so he has more time to socialize with the guests. He advises that it's a heavy appetizer, but so easy and delicious. It is also worthy of a starter before a formal sit-down dinner.

4 (12- to 14-ounce) New York strip steaks

Kosher salt

Obie-Cue's Double Strength Garlic Pepper or your own favorite garlic pepper

Coarsely ground black pepper

Cayenne (optional)

4 tablespoons (½ stick) unsalted butter, melted

Small (slider) buns, for serving (optional)

Sprinkle the steaks with a nice coating of kosher salt and garlic pepper, followed by some black pepper. If you like your steaks with a little kick, dust them lightly with cayenne. Cover and refrigerate for at least 4 hours or overnight.

Before cooking the steaks, allow them to come up to room temperature. This may take up to 1 hour, depending on thickness.

Prepare a hot grill (500° to 550°F).

Place the meat on the grill and close the lid. The cooking time will vary depending on the type of grill you use and the distance between the grate and the fire and the thickness of the steaks. For rare steaks: Grill the first side for 4 minutes, turn, and grill for 3 minutes. For medium-rare steaks: Grill the first side for 5 minutes, turn, and grill for 4 minutes. For medium: Grill the first side for 6 minutes, turn, and grill for 5 minutes. If anyone wants well-done steaks, just make him a hamburger instead.

Remove from the grill and baste with melted butter. Allow to rest for 10 to 15 minutes on a warm plate before slicing. Slice ¼ inch from the short side of the steak. Fan out for presentation, if you like, and serve with the juices or your favorite condiments on small slider buns, if using.

We had a sales meeting dinner at our house. People were there from all over the United States. I smoked ribs, chicken, pork, brisket, and brats. My wife made all the sides and dessert. Everyone was able to experience real Southern barbecue. It was a huge success, and no one left hungry!

—Scott Burton, South Pork

SCOTT AND SUZANNE BURTON, SOUTH PORK

We are a husband and wife team from Madison, Alabama. We started cooking at professional barbecue competitions in 2004. Our team name is South Pork because Scott loves the cartoon *South Park* and the only thing he knew how to cook then was pork. At our first contest at WhistleStop, we got fifth place in pork! We cooked six events that year and were hooked.

To date, we have competed in the United States as far west as Las Vegas, Nevada; as far east as Gaffney, South Carolina; as far north as Springfield, Kentucky; and as far south as Daytona Beach, Florida. We were part of Team ButtRub.com that competed at Grillstock in Bristol, England, and won King of the Grill in 2011. In eight years of cooking, we have racked up ten Grand Championships and fifteen Reserve Grand Championships. We feel that our success is largely due to cooking consistently across all four meats. In 2011, we competed in twenty-four Kansas City Barbeque Society (KCBS) contests with seventeen Top-10 finishes including six first place, two second place, and four third place, which earned us the award for KCBS Team of the Year in Chicken. We also finished twentieth overall out of more than 4,500 professional teams. We were third place in the 2011 Georgia BBQ Championship and second place in the 2011 Alabama Barbecue Association.

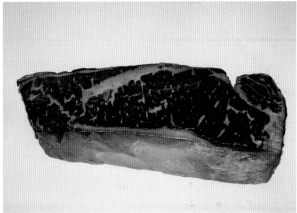

Smoky Jon's Fiery and Frosty Chicken Salad

Serves 12 to 16

With its cool, creamy, spicy taste, this dish is a hit at any backyard barbecue. You can serve it as an appetizer on Ritz crackers or dinner rolls or as an entrée on croissants or bread. Smoky Jon likes to add a little romaine lettuce, Roma tomato, and scallion and serve it as a dinner salad.

2 pounds barbecued boneless, skinless chicken breasts, cut into ½-inch cubes

½ cup salad dressing, such as Miracle Whip

1 to 2 tablespoons cold 2% milk

2 to 3 teaspoons Walkerswood Jamaican Jerk Seasoning

2 to 3 tablespoons diced white onion

Small (slider) buns or crackers, for serving

In a large bowl, combine the chicken, salad dressing, milk, jerk seasoning, and onion and mix well. Chill for at least 1 hour before serving on buns or crackers.

The best backyard barbecue I ever hosted was on Father's Day. The weather was perfect—70°F, sunny, with no wind. I had some prime tenderloin tails that had been dry marinating for 7 days, as well as my mother's famous potato salad, my cold-smoked bacon baked beans, and my mother's malted milk brownies on the menu. The company was great, and we all agreed that it was the nicest time we ever had at a backyard barbecue. It was a very special day for our family, and one I'll never forget.
—Smoky Jon, Smoky Jon's #1 BBQ

SMOKY JON, SMOKY JON'S #1 BBQ

I got involved in competition barbecuing because my family did a lot of backyard charcoal cooking and, while I loved the cooking, I found that I loved eating even more. One day almost 40 years ago, inspired by coverage of the Houston Livestock Show World's Championship Bar-B-Que Contest, I called barbecue legend Billy Bones, who agreed to mentor me. Today I run an award-winning barbecue team, a catering service, a successful restaurant in Madison, Wisconsin, and a sauce business.

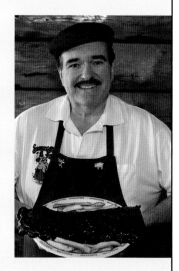

Wildcatters Salsa

Makes 8 to 10 cups

We give you fair warning that your palate should be as tough as a wildcatter to handle the level of fieriness in this salsa. If you like hot salsa that isn't just hot, but is also big on flavor, here's one you'll make over and over again. No wonder it has won so many awards for the Wildcatters!

4 jalapeños, cored, seeded, and diced

4 serrano peppers, cored, seeded, and diced

2 Anaheim peppers, cored, seeded, and diced

1 yellow bell pepper, cored, seeded, and diced

1 orange bell pepper, cored, seeded, and diced

1 medium white onion, diced

1 medium red onion, diced

1 medium yellow onion, diced

8 Roma tomatoes, diced

1 (16-ounce) can diced tomatoes

1 (16-ounce) can pureed tomatoes

2 (16-ounce) cans crushed pineapple, drained

3 cloves garlic, pressed

Juice of 1 lime

2 tablespoons sugar

1 teaspoon ground cumin

½ teaspoon cayenne

¼ cup chopped fresh cilantro

Tortilla chips, for serving

In a large bowl, combine all the ingredients except the cilantro and chips. Mix well. Refrigerate for approximately 1 hour, then add the cilantro and chill for 15 minutes more. Enjoy on your favorite chips.

Our best barbecue bash was on the 4th of July in 2009. The weather was good, the food was awesome, and our daughter's boyfriend was going to propose to her—and everyone but she knew it. With cameras rolling, he got down on one knee and popped the question. Of course she said yes. There were cheers and tears.

—Jeff Brown, Wildcatters

CHAPTER 4: If you take our advice and serve small portions of delicious starters, your guests will be ready to chow down on the main course. This is the moment when it's fun to have a noisemaker such as a cowbell or a triangular chuckwagon dinger to get everyone's attention. That's also when you announce the serving protocol—e.g., sit at a table and be served or line up at the buffet tables, serve yourself, and sit where you wish.

We selected dishes for this chapter that we think will make any backyard barbecue memorable. There is enough variety here to please every palate, and the recipes are easy to follow. Besides three standard contest meats—brisket, ribs, chicken—we chose a burger from Puerto Rico that will have your guests begging for the recipe, plus main dishes featuring beef steaks, lamb, duck, and seafood. Each recipe, in its own way, reflects the personality of the cook. And if that isn't enough, we've given you a brief biography of the cooks in their own words.

Main Dishes

3 Eyz BBQ Pork Roll

Serves 4 to 6

Dan Hixon and 3 Eyz BBQ compete in more than two dozen contests in any given year, and as Dan points out, that's a lot of leftovers. He gave us this recipe, which is one of his favorite ways to use leftover barbecued pulled pork. We pointed out that the recipe had a pretty basic name, and asked him if we should call it something with a little more kick, and Dan said, "Nah, but it is deeeelicious!"

1 (16-ounce) loaf frozen ready-to-bake bread dough, thawed

2 tablespoons 3 Eyz BBQ Rub or your favorite rub

2 cups leftover pulled pork

1 cup shredded pepper Jack cheese

1 cup Sweet Baby Ray's barbecue sauce or your favorite sauce

Heat a cooker to 350°F.

Roll the dough on a lightly floured surface into a circle 12 to 14 inches in diameter.

Sprinkle the rub onto the dough. Fill in the center of the dough circle with the pulled pork and shredded cheese. Wet the dough edges and then fold them over and pinch together. Form the filled dough into a log shape.

Place the log in a foil pan seam side down and place the pan in the cooker. Cover and cook for about 25 minutes, or until the top is a light golden brown. Remove from the cooker and let cool for about 15 minutes, then slice and drizzle with barbecue sauce.

Variations: Add diced peppers and/or hot pepper jelly to the filling.

Brush the top with melted butter and sprinkle with more rub when done.

Use leftover brisket instead of pork.

DAN HIXON, 3 EYZ BBQ

I am pitmaster of the 3 Eyz BBQ competition team. Since 2006, we have competed in more than eighty-five contests across the United States, won four state titles, eight Grand Championships, and more than 220 top-ten awards. We've been featured on TLC's *BBQ Pitmasters*.

It all started with cooking for my friends and family at home in Maryland. I used to fancy myself quite the grill man. I actually used to boil a

rack or two of ribs and cook pulled pork in a slow cooker. I don't recommend those practices now, but a man's gotta start somewhere. I watched cooking shows, and I bought a cheap grill and used to just burn the crap out of everything. At the time, it tasted good, but I never imagined how good barbecue could be. I entered a couple of contests, got sucked in after a couple of awards, and signed up for a cooking class taught by Mr. Paul Kirk. Since that day in 2006, we have been on a tear on the contest circuit.

Squeal of Approval Lemon Pepper Pork Tenderloin

Serves 6 to 8

This is a recipe Squeal of Approval makes at home and in competition. It can be done in the oven or on the smoker/grill.

2 to 4 (1-pound) pork tenderloins

1 (12.7-ounce) bottle Allegro Original Marinade or your favorite marinade

¼ to ½ cup lemon pepper

2 to 4 sprigs fresh rosemary

1 to 2 cups apple juice, for spritzing

Puncture the tenderloins with a fork to allow the marinade to soak in. Place them in a zipper bag with the bottle of marinade. Seal the bag and let sit for 30 minutes.

Heat a cooker or the oven to 350°F.

Remove the tenderloins from the marinade and place them on a small sheet pan. Rub generously with the lemon pepper on all sides. Place the sprigs of rosemary around the tenderloins, then spritz with apple juice.

Place the sheet pan on the grill or in the oven and cook for 30 to 45 minutes, or until the internal temperature reaches 160°F on a meat thermometer. Remove from the grill or oven and let rest for 10 minutes before slicing.

BETSY MASTERS, SQUEAL OF APPROVAL

Our all-female competition barbecue team was formed in 2003. We quickly got everyone's attention by finishing third overall in our first contest. We have been hooked on competition barbecue, backyard barbecue, and everything barbecue ever since. Our smoker repertoire has included a homemade barrel, a Weber Smokey Mountain, Brinkmann, Horizon, and Big Green Egg, and we now cook with a hot pink Jambo. We love to compete, but more than that, we love our barbecue family!

BBQ Freaks Tamarind-Glazed Pork Chops

Serves 8

Jose Bengoa, Yolanda Bolivar, and Gabriel Antunez, the BBQ Freaks of San Juan, Puerto Rico (see page 131), developed this easy method for infusing a sweet clove and nutmeg accent into your next batch of pork chops. Finished with a tamarind glaze, these chops will likely be unlike any your guests have tried before. You can buy tamarind pulp at health food stores and in Asian, Hispanic, and Indian food stores. We advise throwing in a few extra chops for guests who will want seconds. For a variation, try grilling the brined chops over charcoal or gas, followed by smoking at 250°F for 25 to 30 minutes.

TAMARIND GLAZE

1 tablespoon vegetable oil

1 medium yellow onion, chopped

3 cloves garlic

1 sprig fresh thyme

½ cup rum (añejo)

1 cup honey

1 cup tamarind pulp

3 cups beef stock

BRINE

4 quarts water

1 cup sugar

1 cup salt

30 whole cloves

4 whole nutmegs, cracked

PORK CHOPS

8 center-cut pork chops,
   about 2½ inches thick

Kosher salt and cracked black pepper

Granulated garlic, for seasoning

Dried thyme, for seasoning

To make the glaze: Place the vegetable oil in a medium skillet over medium-high heat. Add the onion, garlic, and thyme and cook until the onion and garlic begin to brown, 7 to 10 minutes. Deglaze the pan with the rum and simmer for 4 to 5 minutes to evaporate the alcohol. Stir in the honey and tamarind pulp and cook over medium heat for 5 minutes. Add the beef stock and continue cooking until the liquid is reduced by half. Strain through a sieve. Cover and refrigerate until ready to use.

To brine the pork chops: In a large stockpot, bring to a boil the water, sugar, salt, cloves, and nutmegs. Stir occasionally and cook until the sugar and salt have dissolved. Remove the brine from the heat and add the pork chops. Let cool for 30 minutes, then cover and refrigerate for 24 hours.

Prepare a hot grill for direct cooking, with a cool zone to one side.

Remove the pork chops from the brine, rinse with cold water, and pat dry. Season to your liking with salt, cracked black pepper, granulated garlic, and dried thyme.

Use long-handled tongs and a paper towel dipped in vegetable oil to lightly oil the grate, then place the pork chops over the fire, about 6 inches over the glowing coals. Cook for about 2 minutes on each side. Move the chops to the cool zone, cover the grill, and cook for 5 minutes. Turn, cover the grill, and grill until just cooked through, about 5 minutes more. The meat should register 145°F on a meat thermometer.

Transfer to a serving platter and allow the chops to rest for 10 minutes. While the meat is resting, warm the glaze. Serve the pork chops whole or sliced with the glaze.

Note: You can also make these in the oven. First, sear the chops in very hot oil in a shallow pan for about 5 minutes on each side. Place in a preheated 350°F oven and bake for 25 to 30 minutes or until they register 145°F on a meat thermometer. Let them rest for 10 minutes before serving.

AM & PM Smokers Backyard Campfire Thick-Cut Pork Loin Chops

Serves 4

Phil told us that this recipe harks back to his Boy Scout days. He put his own spin on the original recipe and has prepared this dish many times for backyard barbecue guests and on camping trips. It's what he calls "comfort food 101," cooked on the firebox of his backyard pit.

The combination of meat, beans, onion, and complementary seasonings makes it a complete meal. It is always a big hit.

1 cup finely diced smoked pork jowl or bacon

4 thick-cut pork loin chops

Salt and freshly ground black pepper

All-purpose flour, for dredging

1 medium onion (red, Spanish, whatever you like), thinly sliced

2 cans of your favorite pork and beans or your own baked beans

¼ to ½ cup of your favorite prepared mustard

½ cup ketchup

Cholula hot sauce

½ cup firmly packed dark brown sugar

Heat a bed of coals and place a 12-inch cast-iron Dutch oven over them but not directly in the coals. AM & PM Smokers hang theirs from a tripod over the coals. You can also place the Dutch oven on the firebox of your backyard pit. Make sure your oven is not too close to the fire, to avoid scorching the mixture.

When the Dutch oven is hot, place the jowl in it and cook until the fat is rendered out and the jowl is browned. Remove the crispy bits.

Season the chops with salt and pepper and dredge in the flour. Place the chops in the Dutch oven and cook until browned on both sides. Place half of the sliced onion over the chops, pour the beans over the onion and chops, then place dollops of the mustard, ketchup, hot sauce (as much as you like), and brown sugar on top of the beans. Gently stir in the dollops and place the remaining onion over the layer of beans.

Cover the Dutch oven and simmer until the chops are tender, 1 to 1½ hours.

PHIL AND ROSEMARY MORROW, AM & PM SMOKERS

AM & PM Smokers BBQ Team began like many of the teams throughout the United States. Our two wonderful sons gave Dad a water smoker for Father's Day—the kind you put a water pan in, charcoal, brisket, a rack or two of ribs, some smoke wood on the coals, put the lid on, and wait. Like many, I (Phil) waited and then heard, "Dad, this is some good stuff!!"

I (again, Phil) eventually met people who enticed us into joining the Kansas City Barbeque Society. We think it was around 1993, maybe in Lincoln, Arkansas, when we received our first ribbon in brisket. We went on to win many awards, ribbons, and plaques, including the 1996 American Royal (1st Place, Beans, Side Dish) and 2004 American Royal Open (1st Place, Sausage; 4th Place, Brisket, out of 475 teams). The award that means the most is the 1997 All America Team of the Year. It was given by the Randy Unkenholtz Family in memory of him, a true competitor and an incredible man. This award is given not for a team's point standings but for displaying a true barbecue spirit to fellow competitors.

I (Phil) would also like to convey a heartfelt thank you to Rosemary, my wife and partner for life, our two sons and their wives, and our extended families; also Larry, Carolyn and Gary Wells, Chef Paul, Chef Karen, Chef Richard, Chef Tom (JCCC), Chef John (RIP), Phil (of Smokin' Guns BBQ & Catering), Jay, and on and on and on. AM & PM Smokers could have never ever gotten to this point without your undying support.

Paul Schatte's Head Country II Barbecue Spareribs

Serves 3 to 4

Paul Schatte (see page 29) is known throughout Oklahoma and in the nationwide competition barbecue network as a champion who is second to none. True to his Oklahoma roots, he doesn't brag about his accomplishments. If we're anywhere nearby when Paul is smoking ribs, we are eager to taste the results. We even cut him some slack for using foil. For best results with this recipe, Paul recommends using Head Country All Purpose Championship Seasoning for the rub and your favorite selection of Head Country Bar-B-Q Sauce (Original, Hickory, or Hot) for the baste and for serving on the side.

1 slab pork spareribs, membrane removed, trimmed

¼ cup of your favorite dry barbecue rub

¼ cup of your favorite barbecue sauce, for basting

Your favorite barbecue sauce, for serving

Heat a smoker to 270°F.

Season the ribs lightly with the rub. Keep in mind that pork is a salty meat to begin with and be careful not to overseason. Place the ribs in the smoker away from direct heat, about 20 inches if possible. Cook for 3½ hours, maintaining a cooking temperature of 270°F; wrap in foil and cook for 45 minutes longer.

Remove the ribs from the foil, baste with barbecue sauce, and cook for 15 minutes longer; turn once. Be careful not to scorch. To check for doneness, take one of the larger bones and twist it. If it twists loosely in the meat, the ribs are done.

Remove from the smoker, slice, and serve with your favorite barbecue sauce.

Feeding Friendz Jalapeño Popper Pizza

Serves 4

This Jalapeño Popper Pizza is one of Tim and Wendy Boucher's specialty dishes that's always a hit at their backyard barbecue gatherings and at contests when friends gather to socialize. As Wendy says, "The possibilities are endless." Tim and Wendy like to use ZaGrill (made by Eastman Outdoors). They told us that it's "probably our favorite grilling gadget because it makes perfect pizza every time."

1 recipe prepared pizza dough for a 12- to 14-inch pizza (Feeding Friendz uses what the local grocery store carries)

4 ounces Neufchâtel cheese, softened

2 teaspoons minced garlic

2 scallions, white and green parts, finely chopped

1 tablespoon taco seasoning

¼ cup panko breadcrumbs, plus more for dusting

1 tablespoon olive oil

1 cup marinara sauce

1 cup Monterey Jack cheese

4 jalapeño peppers, cored, seeded, and thinly sliced

1 cup pepper Jack cheese

3 to 4 slices bacon, cooked and crumbled

Prepare a hot grill.

Roll out the dough as thin or thick as you prefer to fit a grill pan. Place the dough on the grill pan.

In a medium bowl, combine the Neufchâtel, garlic, scallions, and taco seasoning and set aside. In a small bowl, toss the panko with half of the olive oil and set aside.

Spread the marinara sauce over the pizza dough. Dust the outer edges with the panko crumbs.

Sprinkle the Monterey Jack cheese over the sauce, then top generously with the sliced jalapeños.

Scatter small dollops of the Neufchâtel mixture over the pizza. Sprinkle with the pepper Jack cheese and bacon pieces. Drizzle the remaining olive oil over the top.

Place the pan on the grill, close the lid, and bake for 10 to 15 minutes, or until the cheese is melted and the crust browned.

TIM AND WENDY BOUCHER, FEEDING FRIENDZ

We have been competing since 2005 and were fortunate to be invited to the Jack Daniel's World Championship Invitational in 2010 and 2011. We do not need a reason to cook and often just call our friends and say, "Come on over—we're trying something new!"

Big Billy's BBQ Country-Style Ribs

Serves 8 to 10

Here's Billy Rodgers's (see page 101) version of a favorite backyard barbecue dish from his childhood. He dedicates it to his mother, Anna G. He cherishes memories of going with her to visit his grandmother in the summertime. Billy said, "Grandmother lived in a small town where everyone still sits on the front porch and waves at you as you drive by, whether they know you or not. Word would get out around town whenever my mother came home to visit. When people found out that she was cooking dinner, the house would fill. Anyone and everyone would come by to get a plate and sit a spell to enjoy each other's company."

RUB

⅓ cup sugar

3 tablespoons seasoned salt

2 tablespoons paprika

1 tablespoon chipotle powder

2 teaspoons granulated garlic

2 teaspoons freshly ground black pepper

½ teaspoon granulated onion

¼ teaspoon ground white pepper

¼ teaspoon cayenne

¼ teaspoon MSG (optional)

SAUCE

¾ cup ketchup

¼ cup maple syrup

¼ cup bourbon

2 tablespoons clover honey

2 tablespoons cider vinegar

2 tablespoons prepared mustard

½ teaspoon salt

¼ teaspoon freshly ground black pepper

¼ teaspoon cayenne

⅛ teaspoon ground white pepper

⅛ teaspoon onion powder

⅛ teaspoon garlic powder

5 pounds country-style pork ribs (see Note)

Vegetable oil

Mix the ingredients for the rub in a small bowl. Using a funnel, place the rub into a shaker. Set aside.

Mix the ingredients for the sauce in a small bowl. Cover and leave at room temperature as this is a cold mix sauce and does not require any cooking.

Heat your smoker to 275°F or, if you are using a grill, set it up for indirect cooking by banking the charcoal to one side.

Season the ribs liberally on both sides with the rub at least 30 minutes before placing them on the grill. Use a wire brush and clean your grates, then lightly oil them.

Place the meat in the smoker or, if you are using a grill, on the opposite side of the coals for indirect cooking. Cook for 3½ to 4 hours, or until the internal temperature registers 195°F on a meat thermometer. You can brush with sauce during the last 10 minutes of cooking or serve it in a small bowl on the side. The finished product will have the texture of a tender steak. Remove the ribs from the cooker and let them rest for 10 to 15 minutes before serving.

Note: Select ribs with a light marbling of fat throughout. This lean meat has a tendency to dry over a long period of smoking, producing a dry product. You should still trim any excess or unwanted fat from the outside.

"I would really get excited when I saw my uncle put his stereo speakers in the backyard, the adults setting the tables with red gingham check tablecloths on them and placing a big galvanized tub filled with ice and such between the tables. Yes! It was cookout time! I used to love to watch everyone try to get that old cast-iron grill fired up to cook homemade oversized burgers, pork chops, and chicken. Mmm, mmm, mmm—I can still smell it as I reminisce.

Here is a recipe that takes me back to those wonderful summer days in my grandmother's backyard. I hope that you enjoy it!"

—Billy Rodgers, Big Billy's BBQ

Rick Naug's Grilled Pizza

Makes enough for 12 to 16 pizzas

These small pizzas from Apple Creek Smokers will feed one or two people, depending on how hungry you are. With this recipe, you can make enough pizza to feed a crowd or have some leftover dough in your freezer for a quick weeknight meal. You can bake the pizzas in the oven, but there's nothing like the flavor and texture of a pizza hot off the grill. By the way: Rick tells us his pizza sauce is also great on pasta. We've tried it, and we agree. It is not as complex as Spagman's sauce (page 86), but it does the job. It is also delicious on grilled provolone cheeseburgers!

CRUST

½ **teaspoon instant yeast**

1½ **teaspoons sugar**

4½ **teaspoons salt**

4½ **cups warm water**

12 **ounces semolina**

3 **pounds high-gluten flour**

Olive oil, for coating

SAUCE

1 **pound ripe Roma tomatoes**

5 **cloves garlic, crushed**

10 **leaves fresh basil, chopped**

1 **tablespoon olive oil**

1 **tablespoon grated low-moisture mozzarella cheese**

Pinch of salt

1 **tablespoon dried oregano, crushed (optional)**

Your favorite shredded cheese and toppings

Make the dough: In the bowl of a stand mixer fitted with a bread hook, combine the yeast, sugar, salt, and warm water and mix on low speed for 3 to 4 minutes. In a large bowl, whisk together the semolina and flour. With the mixer running, slowly add them to the water mixture. Continue mixing until the dough pulls away clean from the sides and bottom of the bowl, 5 to 6 minutes.

Turn the dough onto a cutting board, cover with a clean, lint-free cloth, and let rest for 10 to 15 minutes.

Divide the dough into 12 to 16 (6- to 8-ounce) pieces. Stretch each 2 or 3 times, roll the edges under, and form a ball. Coat the balls with olive oil and place them in a lightly oiled pan. Cover and refrigerate for 5 to 6 hours or overnight. When you're ready to use them, bring them to room temperature.

You can freeze some or all of the dough balls for later use. Coat the outsides of the dough balls with olive oil, place them in a zipper freezer bag, seal tightly, removing any air, and freeze. Bring the dough balls to room temperature before using.

Make the sauce: Preheat the oven to 400°F.

Blanch the tomatoes in boiling water until the skins can be removed easily, 1 to 2 minutes. Transfer them to a sheet pan, add the garlic cloves, and use a potato masher or fork to crush them. Place the pan in the oven and roast until the liquid is reduced by half. Remove from the oven and add the basil and olive oil. Return to the oven for 5 minutes, or until the sauce starts to bubble. Remove from the oven and stir in the mozzarella.

Rick uses a wood-burning pizza oven to bake the pizzas at 600°F, which takes only 4 to 5 minutes to cook. You can preheat your grill to 375° to 425°F.

On a work surface lightly dusted with semolina, press and roll the dough between ⅛ and ¼ inch thick and about 8 inches in diameter. Spread some sauce on the dough round, leaving about ½ inch uncovered around the edges. Season with salt and sprinkle the oregano, if using, on top. Add your favorite cheese and toppings. Lightly dust a pizza peel with semolina, then carefully transfer the pizza to the grill over direct heat. Close the lid and cook until the cheese is melted and the crust begins to turn golden brown, 20 to 30 minutes.

Remove from the grill, slice, and serve.

We like to fire up the pizza oven on our deck. After a brief demo, I turn the cooking over to our guests. Watching first-time pizza cooks apply their budding skills is priceless. Preparing the food becomes the entertainment. The proof is in the laughter. However, never, ever has anyone been unsuccessful in making his or her favorite "pie." And no matter what it looks like, one and all claim it to be the best pizza ever!

—Rick Naug, Apple Creek Smokers

Hector Rivera's Charcoalholics Spicy Coconut and Rum Ribs

Serves 6 to 8

Hector (see page 93) has won first place twice with this recipe. These ribs are so popular with Hector's family and friends that he often serves them at backyard barbecues. Hector told us that the first thing he did upon recovering from an illness that put him in bed for 6 months was to cook these ribs in celebration of a cousin's daughter's first birthday. Lucky girl! We wish we could have teethed on these spicy ribs with a coconut accent when we were infants!

SLATHER

½ cup prepared mustard

¼ cup coconut milk

¼ cup sugar

2 tablespoons rice wine vinegar

2 tablespoons curry paste

¼ cup chili sauce

¼ cup pineapple juice concentrate

1 tablespoon canola oil

¼ cup dark rum

RUB

½ cup turbinado sugar

1 tablespoon salt

½ cup all-purpose seasoning

2 tablespoons five-spice powder

1 teaspoon crushed red pepper

2 tablespoons curry powder

2 teaspoons paprika

¼ cup chili powder

¼ cup garlic powder

2 tablespoons ground cumin

SAUCE

½ cup chili sauce

½ cup ketchup

⅔ cup coconut milk

⅔ cup Coco Lopez coconut cream

3 tablespoons hot curry paste

2 tablespoons barbecue rub

½ cup pineapple concentrate

2 tablespoons soy sauce

2 tablespoons rice wine vinegar

2 tablespoons sriracha sauce

½ cup dark rum

RIBS

4 slabs pork loin back (baby back) ribs or spareribs, membrane removed, trimmed

Coconut water in a spray bottle, for spritzing

Combine the slather ingredients in a bowl and whisk well. Set aside.

Combine the rub ingredients in a small bowl, mix well, and set aside.

Combine the sauce ingredients in a saucepan and cook over medium-low heat for 20 minutes.

Pat the ribs dry. Use a pastry brush to apply the slather. Wrap tightly in plastic or place in a 2-gallon zipper bag and refrigerate overnight.

Three hours before cooking time, remove the ribs from the refrigerator and rub with about 3 tablespoons of the rub.

Heat a cooker to 225°F.

When the cooker is hot, place the ribs on the grate, cover, and cook for about 4 hours (5 hours for spares), spritzing with coconut water every hour. About 45 minutes before the ribs are done, slather with sauce. Slather with sauce again about 15 minutes before the ribs are done. When you can grasp 2 side-by-side ribs and easily pull them apart, remove the ribs from the cooker. Let them rest for 20 minutes before serving.

Dirty Dick's Grilled Baby Back Ribs

Serves 6

We credit Richard Westhaver with being an innovator in helping promote New England competition barbecue into a rapidly growing network of contenders who continue to show up on the awards stage at major contests everywhere. Competing as Dirty Dick and the Legless Wonders, Richard's team (see page 147) has garnered its share of awards. With this recipe, Richard demonstrates an easy way to barbecue baby backs that are high on flavor.

2 slabs (about 3 pounds) pork loin (baby back) ribs, membrane removed, trimmed

4 to 6 tablespoons Dirty Dick's Barbecue Spice (page 147) or your favorite barbecue rub

Apple juice, for spraying

2 cups Dirty Dick's Barbecue Sauce or your favorite barbecue sauce

Rub each side of the ribs with 1 tablespoon of the barbecue spice. Wrap and refrigerate overnight. The next day, before placing the ribs on the grill, reseason them.

Place about 50 briquettes on one side of the grill and light them. Once the coals are ready, throw on 2 handfuls of wood chips. Place the grate over the fire and put the ribs on the side opposite the fire. Close the lid. Open the top and bottom vents on the grill about two-thirds of the way. Place a candy thermometer in the top vent to monitor the temperature. The ideal temperature for cooking the ribs is 350°F.

After 1 hour, open the upper and lower vents to maintain the temperature. Turn the ribs and spray with the apple juice. After 2 hours, when the ribs are done, they will be flexible and the end of the bone will be exposed ½ inch or so.

Remove the ribs from the grill and coat both sides with barbecue sauce, about ½ cup per side. Then wrap the ribs in aluminum foil and seal tightly. Place in a warm spot for 30 minutes. Unwrap and apply more sauce before serving if desired.

U SAW IT HERE

Jeff Brinker's Washington Baby Back Ribs

Serves 6 to 8

We reconstructed Jeff's recipe from notes he gave us on how he cooked these ribs for some blue ribbons. Jeff (see page 84) calls them "Washington Ribs" in reference to his Washington, Missouri, hometown. Jeff's favorite product ingredient sources—from Chandler, Oklahoma; Ville Platte, Louisiana; and Perry, Missouri—exemplify today's barbecue spirit: we are many and separate, but one and united.

1 teaspoon Accent Seasoning or your favorite flavor enhancer (especially if you are non-MSG-tolerant), plus more for finishing

2 cups Butcher BBQ Honey BBQ Rub or your favorite rub

4 slabs pork loin (baby back) ribs

¼ cup Slap Ya Mama or your favorite dry Cajun seasoning

1 cup firmly packed brown sugar

½ cup ginger ale

¼ cup soy sauce

2 cups Blues Hog Barbecue Sauce or your favorite barbecue sauce

1 bottle squeezable margarine, such as Parkay

Salt

Chopped fresh parsley, for serving

Heat a cooker to 265°F.

Combine the Accent seasoning and 1 cup of the barbecue rub in a bowl and stir together. Apply to both sides of the slabs, followed with a light sprinkling of Cajun seasoning on the back (bony) side of each slab.

Combine the brown sugar, ginger ale, and soy sauce in a bowl and whisk well. Slather on both sides of the slabs, followed by a slather of barbecue sauce on the meaty sides of the slabs.

Place each slab on a piece of heavy-duty aluminum foil big enough to wrap and seal the slab. Apply some squeezable margarine and rub onto both sides of the slabs. Seal the foil, then double-wrap with another piece of foil and seal tightly.

Place the slabs separately, not stacked, in your cooker, meat side up. Cook for 1½ hours, then turn the slabs meat side down and cook for 2 more hours.

Remove the slabs from the cooker, unwrap, and let sit for 15 minutes. Transfer to a cutting board, brush the sauce on both sides, and let rest for another 10 minutes. Slice into individual ribs, place on a platter, and sauce lightly. Season with salt and more Accent if desired. Garnish with chopped parsley and serve.

QUAU Prime Rib

Serves 18 to 24

When you want to serve a main dish that is guaranteed to make your nonvegan guests feel like they're in omnivore heaven, prime rib is the way to go. Be sure the occasion and guest list merit it, however, as it is expensive. That is especially the case when you take Mike Wozniak's advice and spring for Wagyu prime rib. Mike told us that Wagyu delivers unbelievable results compared to other breeds. QUAU has made this dish at contests such as the American Royal and The Jack, and it has become the centerpiece of their family Christmas dinners, where the serving platter at the end of the meal is empty, save for some remnants of fat and crust.

1 (12-pound) boneless prime rib, trimmed of excess fat

½ cup dried rosemary leaves, crushed

½ cup dried minced garlic

¾ cup kosher salt

1 (15-ounce) bottle Lea & Perrins Worcestershire sauce

Trim off some of the prime rib's tail (the portion of the prime rib that tapers to a slender point, comprised primarily of fat). Push the prime rib into as round a shape as possible; then use 6 to 7 lengths of butcher's twine to tie the roast into the round shape. The round shape will help the roast cook more evenly.

Place the roast on a cutting board or baking sheet. Mix the rosemary, dried garlic, and salt together, then add enough Worcestershire to make a thick but liquidy slather. Apply it to the exterior of the roast. Place the roast on a piece of plastic wrap approximately twice as long as the roast. Pour whatever slather remains in the pan onto the roast. Wrap the roast with several layers of plastic wrap and refrigerate for about 24 hours, turning every 6 hours or so.

Four or five hours before cooking, remove the roast from the refrigerator and allow it to come to room temperature.

The key to excellent prime rib is cooking extremely hot to develop a crust and sear in the juices. QUAU likes to cook the roast in its barbecue pit's firebox, which is approximately 450°F. Heat your firebox to that temperature and prepare it for indirect cooking.

Place the roast on the cooker away from the coals. Depending on the size of the roast, cook for 1 hour and 30 minutes to 1 hour and 45 minutes, turning occasionally to avoid burning. Check the internal temperature in the middle of the thickest part of the roast. Once it is close to 120°F, move the roast to the cooking chamber of the pit, set to 275° to 300°F.

Once the internal temperature hits 128°F, remove the roast from the cooker and place on a cutting board to rest for 20 to 25 minutes. Cut the twine and slice the roast into portions. The ends of the roast will be medium and the inner cuts medium-rare.

MIKE AND BETH WOZNIAK, QUAU

I (Mike) have always liked to cook. We entered our first competition, a rib contest, in 2000. Beth and I enjoyed it and entered another rib burn a few weeks later. Mike and Teresa Lake of Rock River Barbeque happened to be vending at that event. Mike told me all about the Kansas City Barbeque Society and the Illinois State BBQ Championship in Shannon, Illinois. He further explained that at KCBS comps, teams cook chicken, ribs, pork butt, and beef brisket. I knew what chicken and ribs were, but the only brisket I had had was of the corned beef variety. And what the hell was a pork butt?

Early the next year Beth and I took a Certified Barbeque Judge class, and we cooked our first KCBS contest in June of 2001. It was a lot harder than we thought! In Shannon, Illinois, that year, we got a ribbon in sausage, and at the last contest we cooked in 2001 we took third in chicken—our first award in the main categories. We were hooked!

Paradise Cow Bell Hell Prime Rib

Serves 6 to 8

When Wagyu prime rib (see page 68) doesn't fit your budget, here's a less pricey alternative that will have your guests dancing on the beach. Ron and Bonnie use a top-quality domestic breed and an easy combination of seasonings and cooking techniques that result in an outstanding main dish. Ron and Bonnie are Canadians by birth and Sugarloaf Key, Florida, snowbirds by choice. When Ron and Bonnie crossed wakes as fishers on the key with Wicked Good Maine Barbecuer DennyMike Sherman, they got hooked on a new passion: barbecue. He taught them how to barbecue, shared some of his awesome seasonings with them, and now he says they're good enough to rival him and anyone else in a contest! Try this recipe and you'll agree.

½ cup DennyMike's Cow Bell Hell or your own favorite spicy rub, plus more for rubbing the meat

2 cups water

1 (8- to 10-pound) bone-in prime rib

⅓ cup olive oil

6 to 8 cloves garlic

⅓ cup minced fresh rosemary leaves

¾ cup apple juice

¼ cup Jack Daniel's whiskey

Place the rub in a piece of cheesecloth and tie it up with string. Put the water into a bowl and immerse the cheesecloth bag in the water for 30 minutes, squeezing the bag several times to infuse the water with spice. Use a meat injector to inject the meat with the brine in various locations. Set aside.

Place the olive oil, garlic, and rosemary in a sauté pan and sauté over low heat to infuse the oil with rosemary and garlic. Be careful not to burn the garlic. Let cool.

Place the apple juice and Jack Daniel's in a spray bottle and shake lightly to mix. Set aside.

70

Remove the prime rib from the brine and use a basting brush to coat it with the infused oil. Sprinkle generously with DennyMike's Cow Bell Hell or your own favorite spicy rub. Wrap tightly with plastic wrap and refrigerate overnight.

About 2 hours before cooking, remove the prime rib from the refrigerator and let it come to room temperature.

Preheat a cooker to low to medium heat (300°F).

Place the meat on the grate bone side down, close the lid, and cook for 2 hours. Switch to the smoke setting (see Note) and cook for an additional hour, spritzing occasionally with the apple juice mixture.

Switch the smoke setting back to medium and finish cooking to your desired temperature (135°F for medium-rare), about 1 hour more, spritzing occasionally with the apple juice mixture.

Remove from the grill, cover loosely with foil, and let rest for 15 minutes before carving.

RON AND BONNIE COFFIN, SUGARLOAF KEY PELLET POOPERS

We are from Tide Head, New Brunswick, Canada, but for the last 14 years have also called Sugarloaf Key, Florida, home. We love the weather in the Keys for the winter months but love our summer and fall in Canada. We met barbecue aficionado and icon from Maine DennyMike Sherman while he was visiting a mutual friend and have fallen in love with his spices and sauces. DennyMike's products are the best!

Note: Pellet cookers (or pellet poopers, as they are sometimes affectionately called) have a smoke setting that gives you more smoke. If you're using a standard grill or cooker (aka stick burner), just follow the directions as written, less the smoke setting.

Bone Doctors BBQ Rx Baby Backs

Serves 2 to 4

There are barbecue champions who win competitions, and there are barbecue champions who make it possible for barbecue champions to compete or judge. That would be Dr. Scott Cook, who improved our quality of life immeasurably by giving Paul new knees and Ardie a new right hip. To us, Scott Cook is a champion! We asked him to team up with his dad, Mike Scott, in Houston, and develop a recipe, and they sent this prescription. Ardie, who is mostly a pepper-and-salt-is-enough pitmaster, agrees that this is a superior rub on a slab of ribs—or butts, breasts, and thighs too!

RX RIB RUB

1½ cups packed dark brown sugar

1 tablespoon Lawry's Seasoned Salt

1 tablespoon coarsely ground black pepper

1 tablespoon five-spice powder

2 tablespoons garlic powder

2 tablespoons onion powder

2 tablespoons Hungarian paprika

2 tablespoons dried thyme, crushed

1 tablespoon dried rosemary, crushed

1 tablespoon ground allspice

RIBS

1 slab pork loin (baby back) ribs, membrane removed, trimmed

Apple juice, for spritzing

Combine all the rub ingredients in a small bowl and mix thoroughly. Season the ribs on both sides with the rub and wrap them tightly in plastic or place them in a 2-gallon zipper bag and refrigerate overnight.

Heat a smoker to 225° to 250°F using hickory, post oak, or pecan.

Place the ribs in the smoker and cook for 3 hours, spritzing with apple juice every 45 minutes. After 3 hours, check to see if the meat is drawing back from the end of the rib bone. It should be doing so about ⅛ inch.

Remove the ribs from the smoker, wrap in foil, and return them to the smoker for 1 to 2 hours, or until they reach your desired tenderness. Remove from the smoker, let rest for 10 minutes, then unwrap and serve.

MIKE AND SCOTT COOK, BONE DOCTORS

My (Scott's) barbecue passion began with my dad. He always had something on the smoker when I was growing up, so my interest was, at least initially, mainly in eating barbecue. When I left for college and then medical school, I learned how to barbecue out of absolute necessity in order to feed my eating pursuits! I still call my dad for advice on all things related to cooking. The only time I have been able to combine my passions for medicine and barbecue came when my brother Deke graduated from college in Texas. My dad borrowed a smoker from a friend in order to do a whole hog. The smoker was huge—you had to climb up a ladder to get to the grill, and the lid was counterweighted with 200 pounds so that a mere mortal could get it open! My dad fell off the grill, breaking three ribs, prior to the party. I wrapped him up, prescribed some medicine, and "got him back in the game"! Needless to say, I'll never forget how the hog was so tender and my dad was so tough!

I'LL NEVER FORGET HOW THE HOG WAS SO TENDER AND MY DAD WAS SO TOUGH!

Chris Lilly's Flank Steak and Shiitake Yakitori

Makes 12 to 14 skewers

When Chris Lilly is at the grill and says to you, "Come on back and have a bite when this is ready," he's not making polite idle talk. Take him seriously. Ask him when it will be ready and make a point of being there. Chris, with father-in-law Don McLemore and the Big Bob Gibson competition barbecue team, has brought home so many contest cooking and sauce awards to his hometown of Decatur, Alabama, that we've lost count. Chris has honed his culinary skills to reach far beyond the basic superb down-home flavors of Alabama barbecued pork and chicken. This grilled flank steak recipe is a perfect marriage of authentic Asian flavors and grilling techniques. If you've ever enjoyed grilled meat skewers at an Asian farmers' market—Guangzhou, for example—this dish will put some good memories and wow in your mouth. Chris's version is second to none!

28 shiitake mushroom caps

MARINADE

¾ cup soy sauce

¾ cup mirin (rice wine)

½ cup sugar

¼ cup water

Juice of ½ lime

1 tablespoon chopped fresh cilantro

1 clove garlic, minced

¾ teaspoon peeled, grated fresh ginger

⅛ teaspoon hot red pepper flakes

STEAK

1 (1½- to 2-pound) flank steak

1 bunch scallion tops

1 teaspoon salt

1 teaspoon freshly ground black pepper

Place 12 to 14 (4-inch) skewers in water to soak.

Cut the shiitake mushroom caps in half and place them in a mixing bowl. In a medium saucepan, combine the marinade ingredients and bring to a simmer; simmer for 10 minutes. Remove from the heat and pour the hot liquid over the mushroom caps. Marinate for 20 minutes.

Cut the flank steak across the grain into ¼-inch strips. Cut the scallion tops into 1-inch pieces.

Remove the mushrooms from the marinade and set the marinade aside. Use a skewer to pierce the flank steak at the end of the strip. Next pierce a piece of mushroom cap, followed by a scallion top. Weave the flank steak strip around the mushroom and scallion and continue skewering mushroom, scallion, and flank steak until the steak strip ends. Lightly season the skewers with salt and pepper.

Preheat a hot grill. Dip each skewer into the leftover marinade and place on the grill over direct heat. Grill for 2 minutes on each side, or until the steak browns. Remove the skewers from the grill and serve.

CHRIS LILLY, BIG BOB GIBSON BAR-B-Q COMPETITION COOKING TEAM

My barbecue career began in 1992, when I started working at the world-famous Big Bob Gibson Bar-B-Q restaurant in Decatur, Alabama. I am now vice president, executive chef, and partner, operating two company-owned restaurants and a franchise in Monroe, North Carolina.

I also serve as head chef of the award-winning Big Bob Gibson Bar-B-Q Competition Cooking Team, winner of eleven world barbecue championships, including three Memphis in May Grand Championships. We have also won the American Royal Invitational and eight state barbecue grand championships across the Southeast. Our team has even won abroad, capturing the Grand Championship at the 2003 International Jamaican Jerk Southern Barbecue Cook-Off.

I have been a guest chef for ten years running at the Food Network's South Beach Wine and Food Festival and have served twice as guest chef at the James Beard Foundation and the American Institute of Wine & Food. The National Pork Board recognized me as a Celebrated Chef, and my book, *Big Bob Gibson's BBQ Book*, was named Book of the Year by the National Barbecue Association. I have also been featured in a number of magazines and other publications, and I have appeared on a number of television shows. In 2005 I was cocreator, executive producer, and host of The All-Star BBQ Showdown for the Outdoor Life Network (OLN). In 2006, I became cocreator and executive producer of the BBQ Championship Series on Versus Network.

Smoke in Da Eye Grilled Coffee-Coriander-Rubbed New York Strip Steak

Serves 4

We can always count on Clint Cantwell to come up with flavor profiles that, at first glance, make us blink like we just got smoke in our eyes. Here he's done it again by rubbing steak with coffee, paprika, and coriander—some of the hottest seasonings out there now. It opens up some new flavors you might not have thought of, but they work!

COFFEE-CORIANDER RUB

2 tablespoons ground coffee

3 tablespoons smoked paprika

1½ tablespoons coriander seeds, lightly toasted and ground

½ teaspoon dry mustard

1 teaspoon coarsely ground black pepper

2 tablespoons kosher salt

STEAKS

4 New York strip steaks, about 1½ inches thick

¼ cup extra virgin olive oil

Mix all the rub ingredients together and set aside.

Remove the steaks from the refrigerator and allow them to come to room temperature for about 30 minutes. Meanwhile, heat a grill to high, placing the majority of the coals and a couple (optional) fist-sized wood chunks in the center of the grill to create a cool zone on the outer edges.

Once the steaks have come to room temperature, coat all sides with the olive oil; then season generously with the coffee-coriander rub. Place the steaks in the center of the grill, cover, and cook for 3 minutes. Flip and grill, covered, for another 3 minutes. Flip and cook each side for an additional 2 to 3 minutes, until they reach your desired level of doneness (145° to 150°F for medium-rare and 150° to 160°F for medium according to the USDA. Remember, however, that the meat will rise in temperature as much as 10 degrees as it rests). Remove from the grill and allow to rest for at least 5 minutes so that the juices have time to redistribute and don't end up all over your serving platter or cutting board.

CLINT CANTWELL,
SMOKE IN DA EYE

Since I'm from Texas, barbecue and grilling are in my blood. However, it wasn't until I met my wife in the late nineties that I realized you can actually spend a ton of money trying to show that you've got the outdoor cooking skills to run with the best of the best. And you might get a plastic trophy to boot!

My wife is a Memphis native, and her parents had a beautiful house that looked out over the annual Memphis in May World Championship Barbecue Contest. Every year, we would plan our visits around the contest schedule and I would spend as much time possible meeting teams and absorbing information.

Fast-forward to 1996 and a contest called Grill Kings held roughly ten miles from my home in Long Island, New York. I pulled together a few friends, signed up for the grilling portion of the contest, and gave birth to the Smoke in Da Eye (www.smokeindaeye.com) team name. While we didn't win that day, we held our own, and I signed up for a full Kansas City Barbeque Society contest a few weeks later. Even after that experience (a rain-soaked mud fest complete with a runaway canopy and medium-rare brisket) I continued to refine my recipes and competition strategy until I was actually about to win some categories and, eventually, some contests. Today I do roughly 6 to 8 barbecue and grilling contests a year, which, in addition to my duties as the editor of Grilling.com, is just enough to keep my competitive fire burning.

Que's Your Daddy Steak Mudega

Serves 6 to 8

Our first question when we saw the title of this recipe was "What is mudega?" We didn't find a definition, but we traced the use of the word to the Italian neighborhood in St. Louis known as "The Hill." Steak Mudega as served in restaurants there is prepared in the manner shared here as Doc Richardson's (see page 32) version. The common ingredient that makes it mudega is a melted white cheese on the steak, covered with a creamy mushroom sauce. The cheese of choice in St. Louis is a processed cheese known as Provel. It is made from cheddar, Swiss, and provolone, and its low melting point makes it ideal for this steak. Doc's steak is in the Italian tradition of The Hill. We love it and think you and your guests will love it too. Charcoal grilling is a perfect complement to the Italian flavor profile in this steak. Yum!

MARINADE

½ tablespoon olive oil

½ cup dry sherry

2 tablespoons A.1 Steak Sauce

2 tablespoons Italian seasoned breadcrumbs

2 tablespoons grated Parmesan cheese

2 teaspoons minced fresh garlic

Freshly ground black pepper

STEAKS

3 to 4 (1½-inch-thick) rib eye steaks

SAUCE

4 tablespoons (½ stick) butter

1 (8-ounce) package fresh white button mushrooms, sliced

3 cups strong chicken broth

1 cup white wine

1 tablespoon lemon juice

Pinch of white pepper

1 tablespoon cornstarch

4 teaspoons cold water

¼ cup heavy cream

2 cups Italian seasoned breadcrumbs

3 to 4 slices Provel, provolone, or any other mild white cheese (see Note)

To make the marinade: Place all the ingredients in a 2-gallon freezer bag. Add the rib eyes, seal the bag tightly, and gently toss to coat. Marinate for a minimum of 2 hours or up to overnight, if possible.

To make the sauce: Melt the butter in a large saucepan over medium-high heat and sauté the mushrooms until halfway tender. Add the chicken broth, white wine, lemon juice, and white pepper and heat to a simmer. In a small bowl, combine the cornstarch and cold water, then whisk them into the simmering sauce mixture. Stir in the cream and continue to cook until the sauce begins to thicken, stirring constantly. Keep the sauce warm.

Prepare a very hot grill. Dredge the marinated steaks in Italian breadcrumbs. Place over the hot coals and cook for 3 minutes. Turn each steak a quarter turn to create grill marks and cook for 3 to 4 minutes more. Flip and cook for 3 minutes.

Turn each steak another quarter turn and cook for 3 to 4 minutes longer, or until they reach your desired doneness or the steaks reach an internal temperature of 145° to 150°F for medium-rare.

Place the steaks in a pan, put the cheese on top, close the grill, and wait 5 minutes or more for the cheese to melt. Plate and ladle the sauce over the steaks. Serve immediately.

Note: Although Provel is not easy to find except in St. Louis, you can ask your local grocer or cheese monger to order some for you from Swiss-American Inc. in St. Louis.

Flyboy Brisket

Serves 4 to 6

Here's another sure-to-please backyard brisket recipe. This one is from Steve Renfro of Flyboy, Head Country's friendly Kansas neighbor, less than a hundred road miles north of Ponca City. This one features minimal seasonings that do a great job of complementing the natural umami flavor in the beef. We recommend oak or pecan chunks for your smoke. Flyboy recommends a whole packer brisket or a thick (5 pounds or more) brisket flat end for best results.

1½ teaspoons coarsely
  ground black pepper

1½ teaspoons garlic salt

1½ teaspoons seasoned salt,
  such as Lawry's

1 (4- to 5-pound) beef brisket flat,
  trimmed of excess fat (see Note)

In a small bowl, mix the pepper, garlic salt, and seasoned salt, then season the fat side of the brisket with the mixture. Flip the brisket over and season the meat side. Cover and let sit for about 1 hour at room temperature.

Preheat your cooker (or oven) to 270°F. If you are cooking over charcoal, you can add some dry wood chunks during the cooking process (about 1 chunk every 15 minutes for the first couple of hours). Place the brisket on the grate opposite the heat source and cook for about 4 hours. When the surface starts drying out, spray with water (or apple juice, beer, or whatever you like) very carefully. You don't want to wash off the seasoning. You will need to do this every 20 minutes or so until the brisket starts to render the fat. The fat will then keep the surface moist.

At about 4 hours, the crust on the brisket should be dark brown to partially black. Wrap the brisket in a double layer of 18-inch-wide heavy-duty aluminum foil. The foil needs to be a little more than twice as long as the brisket so it will reach all the way around and still have foil to roll up tight around the meat on all sides.

Once the meat is in the foil, it won't get any more smoke, so you can finish it in your oven if you like. Just put the meat in a pan in a 270°F oven.

Whether on the cooker or in the oven, cook the brisket for another 2½ to 4 hours, checking every 30 minutes, until the core temperature is 190°F on a meat thermometer. Remove it from the cooker and open the foil to allow it to cool down. If you do not do this, the meat will continue to cook and may get too soft to slice. This is a good time to brush the meat with some sauce, which will keep the crust from getting hard and help a little with the cooldown.

Remove the brisket from the foil and place it on a cutting board. It will have lots of juices running out. If mealtime is a couple of hours away, you can just leave the brisket in the foil and wrap it back up once the meat has cooled.

The meat needs to cool for 20 minutes or so, until you can hold your finger against it for a few seconds without saying things that you will have to explain to your children when they get older. Do not slice until it has cooled down. The meat will be juicier and more tender if you wait.

Note: The flat cut has minimal fat and is usually more expensive than the more flavorful point cut, which has more fat. Trim off all the fat from the meat side of the meat. Flip it over and trim the excess fat from the bottom, leaving about ⅛ inch of fat there.

STEVE RENFRO, FLYBOY BBQ

Flyboy BBQ began in 2010 after many years of cooking barbecue. My first attempt was back around 1992, with an inexpensive smoker from a home supply company. I knew very little about the art of barbecue, so my finished product was not very good, and the cooker eventually went into the trash. About five years later I bought an offset smoker and tried again. A few attempts with the new cooker produced the same results as before.

A few years later I found a book that had a story about how a cooking team prepared its brisket. I brushed the dust off the smoker, lit it up, and tried a brisket. Success! So I tried the same technique on a shoulder. Success again.

I had always thought it would be fun to go to a contest to watch people cook, smell the smoke, and eat the food, but I figured I would have to go to Kansas City or Memphis to do so. Then, in late 2009, TLC broadcast *BBQ Pitmasters*. The show got me to see if there were any contests near me, and I found five within driving distance. So I bought a 325-gallon tank and started the construction of my new smoker. Two months later, I took a backyard barbecue cooking class. In another month, we went to our first contest.

In our first two years of competitions, we were in seventeen contests, got called at fifteen of those contests, and won three of them. We got two Grand Champions and three Reserve Grand Champions in one season alone. At the 2011 Jack Daniel's World Championship, we got a call for our ribs. Am I hooked? Oh, yeah!

Paul Schatte's Head Country II Barbecue Brisket

Serves 6 to 8

When you're looking for a great brisket recipe to wow your backyard barbecue guests, what better place to get it than from a legendary barbecue champ in a major beef-producing state? Paul Schatte (see page 29) also co-owns and is general manager of Head Country, a favorite brand of barbecue sauces, marinades, and rubs in Oklahoma and the world. We're big fans of Head Country, as are many other Kansas Citians. Paul's procedure for homestyle backyard barbecue brisket is less complex than his secret competition mode, but your guests will declare it a winner!

1 (4- to 5-pound) beef brisket flat, trimmed of excess fat (see Note)

Head Country All Purpose Championship Seasoning or your favorite seasoning

¼ cup plus ⅓ cup Head Country Premium Marinade or your favorite marinade

Head Country Bar-B-Q Sauce or your favorite sauce

Season the entire brisket generously with all-purpose seasoning and place it in a large pan. Pour about 2 tablespoons of the marinade over the top of the lean side of the brisket and massage it into the muscle. Turn the brisket over and pour about 2 tablespoons more marinade on that side and massage it in. This step can be done the night before you are going to cook the brisket. Just tightly wrap and refrigerate overnight, then bring it to room temperature (1 to 1½ hours) before cooking.

Build a fire with 5 pounds of hardwood charcoal and pecan wood 10 to 12 inches below the grate. If you can measure the heat, it should be 275°F. Allow the fire to burn for about 30 minutes.

Place the brisket fat side up on the grate. Cover and cook for 3 hours. At that time the internal temperature should read 150° to 160°F. Remove the brisket from the cooker and place it on a double layer of heavy-duty aluminum foil. Pull the edges of foil up to create a bowl shape. Pour the remaining ⅓ cup of marinade on the brisket and wrap tightly.

Increase the cooking temperature to 300°F, return the brisket to the cooker, and cook for 3½ hours longer. The internal temperature of the brisket should read 190°F when tender. For fall-apart tenderness, cook until the internal temperature reaches 203° to 205°F. Remove the brisket from the cooker, but leave it in the foil. Slightly open the foil and allow the meat to reabsorb its natural juices for 25 minutes.

Remove from the foil, slice across the grain, and serve with your favorite sauce.

Note: The flat cut has minimal fat and is usually more expensive than the more flavorful point cut, which has more fat.

Gaelic Gourmet Smoked Corned Beef Brisket

Serves 6 to 8

There are many ways to cook corned beef, as you'll discover on Snake Saturday in North Kansas City each year the weekend before Saint Patrick's Day. Given his Irish credentials and barbecue prowess, we asked Marty Lynch, the Gaelic Gourmet, to share his secret to turning out a smoked corned beef brisket to perfection. You'll raise a toast of Irish whiskey or beer to this one! We suggest using hickory, pecan, oak, or your favorite wood chips for smoking. It takes a couple of days, but your guests will never forget the flavor.

1 (5-pound) corned beef brisket flat

2 tablespoons olive oil

⅓ cup of your favorite barbecue rub

Mustard or barbecue sauce, for serving

Soak the brisket in water to cover overnight, or boil it for 45 minutes to reduce the salt content.

When the brisket is cool enough to handle (if boiled), rinse it and pat dry with paper towels. Apply oil on all surfaces, then sprinkle all over with barbecue rub. Wrap in plastic wrap or foil and refrigerate overnight.

Remove the brisket from the refrigerator and let it come to room temperature, about 1 hour. Set up a smoker and bank the coals on each side.

Smoke for 4 to 6 hours, or until tender and the internal temperature reaches 185° to 195°F on a meat thermometer. Remove from the smoker and let rest for 20 minutes. Slice the meat against the grain and enjoy as is or with your favorite mustard or barbecue sauce.

MARTY LYNCH, GAELIC GOURMET

At work one Monday a friend came up to me and said he was impressed because at Crown Center in Kansas City he saw people cooking for the American Royal Invitational and wanted to do it the next year so we could "drink beer and play with fire." We entered and have had the time of our lives from then on. I enjoyed it so much that after retirement I went to culinary school and have been cooking as a second career since then. Each contest is a new chance to outdo myself, and with the wonderful friends I have in the barbecue world, that is easy to accomplish.

Jeff Brinker's Easy Wagyu Chili

Serves 10 to 12

JEFF BRINKER, B&B BBQ

I've always been a cook. My mom cooked for the Danforth family (former principal shareholders in Ralston-Purina) at a local wildlife farm they owned, and I watched her every day in the kitchen. Barbecue, however, was totally foreign to me. My dad couldn't grill a steak or barbecue a pork steak to save his life. In my mid-twenties, as a sales manager, I traveled to barbecue places such as North Carolina, Memphis, and Kansas City. After I moved home to Washington, Missouri, I started toying with barbecue on a Brinkmann smoker from Ace Hardware. I took my samples to a convenience store for honest opinions. When I started to hit on good pulled pork, I sold some at the store. It was a hit, and I bought a larger pit on a trailer.

Barbecue contests looked like fun, so I bought Paul Kirk's Championship BBQ as well as a book by John Willingham, practiced a bit, and dove in. We had cooked and won a couple of chili cook-offs, so I thought, How hard could this barbecue thing be? It was a different ball game. My first contest was a seventy-team event at a store in Kansas City. We struggled, but we got a fourth-place call in wild game. We were hooked. Fifty-plus contests later, we have a wall full of ribbons, three great sponsors, a couple of Grand Championships, several Reserve Grand Championships, many first-place ribbons and, above all, some of the best friends on the planet.

Meat from Japanese cattle mated with Angus cattle—Wagyu—has become popular with barbecuers who are looking for a competitive edge. It is easier to smoke a tender brisket from Wagyu beef due to extensive marbling throughout the muscle. Wagyu brisket is pricey, so you'll not want to waste it. Jeff's easy recipe will give you a value-added chili that your guests will love.

1 pound fresh (uncooked) beef chorizo

Salt and freshly ground black pepper

2 pounds Wagyu brisket trimmings, coarsely ground

1 (28-ounce) can crushed tomatoes

40 ounces hot chili beans (or mild if you prefer)

¼ cup chili powder

1 teaspoon dried Greek oregano, crushed

2 tablespoons dried minced onion

1 teaspoon granulated garlic

1 (12-ounce) can V8 vegetable juice

¼ cup pickled jalapeño juice

¼ cup loosely packed brown sugar

1 teaspoon ground cumin

Cayenne

Place the chorizo in a large skillet over medium-high heat and season with salt and pepper. Use a spatula to break it up; then cook until browned, 3 to 5 minutes. Drain well and transfer to a large nonreactive pan over medium heat.

Add the remaining ingredients and bring to a boil. Reduce the heat and simmer, uncovered, for at least 1 hour, stirring occasionally, before serving.

KCass Smoked Turkey Jambalaya

Serves 8 regular people or 4 Cajuns

Rich Tuttle's dad, C. E. "Ol' Smokey" Tuttle, gave us a fantastic smoked turkey recipe years ago for the original *Kansas City Barbeque Society Cookbook*. It has been a family favorite of many KCBS members ever since. Now Ol' Smokey's son has tweaked his dad's recipe into a turkey jambalaya dish that will put some smoke and fire in your mouth and a big smile on your face, guaranteed!

1 pound smoked sausage, sliced

1 medium yellow onion, chopped

1 red bell pepper, cored, seeded, and chopped

1 yellow bell pepper, cored, seeded, and chopped

4 cloves garlic, minced

1 medium celery stalk, chopped

2 cups long-grain white rice

3 to 4 cups turkey stock

1 pound smoked turkey, diced or chopped

Salt and freshly ground black pepper

Louisiana Hot Sauce, for serving

Garlic bread, for serving

In a large cast-iron skillet or pan over medium to medium-high heat, cook the smoked sausage to render enough fat to sauté the vegetables. Add the onion, peppers, garlic, and celery and cook until tender, 5 to 7 minutes. Before all the liquid is evaporated, add the rice and cook until the liquid is absorbed and the vegetables are tender. Add the turkey stock, bring to a boil, and immediately reduce the heat to a simmer. Cover and cook for about 25 minutes. The rice should be al dente. Add the smoked turkey and cook for an additional 5 minutes. Season to taste with salt and pepper.

Serve with Louisiana Hot Sauce and garlic bread.

RICH AND BUNNY TUTTLE, KCASS BBQ

Rich and Bunny Tuttle established KCass BBQ team in 1987. They have become lifetime members of the Kansas City Barbeque Society, and they are also KCBS Certified Master Judges, KCBS Contest Representatives, and KCBS Certified Barbecue Instructors. Their first love is cooking competitions and camaraderie with their barbecue family, and they see their future in active roles in the barbecue society. They sell their own KCass Barbecue Sauce, which won high awards in the Diddy-Wa-Diddy barbecue sauce contest and was selected Tastemaster's Choice by contest founder Ardie Davis (aka Remus Powers). They are currently working on their own barbecue cookbook to finally earn their PhB (a doctorate in barbecue at Greasehouse University).

CHARLIE'S BALLS
WITH ED'S SAUCE
AND PASTA

When Ed Tonino (see page 19) took Chef Paul's pitmaster class at the Raitt Homestead Farm Museum in Elliot, Maine, prior to the Mainely Grillin' & Chillin' State BBQ Competition, he was determined to show Paul the best barbecue sauce he had ever tasted. When it was time to wow the Baron, Ed eagerly awaited the reaction. He turned red when Paul remarked, "This would be really good on spaghetti." Paul nicknamed Ed "Spagman." After getting past his disappointment, Ed was amused, and proud of his new nickname. He and his Redneck Caviar teammate, Frank Kondor, even tried it on pasta and liked it. They have since tweaked the recipe to make a fantastic Redneck Caviar secret barbecue sauce.

After becoming a fan of Ed's sauce at the Mainely Grillin' & Chillin' contest, Ardie discovered some delicious meatballs in a small-town Minnesota café. At first bite he thought, These would go really well with Spagman Sauce!

When "Charlie's Balls" are the daily special at the Heartland Kitchen and Café in downtown Crosby, Minnesota, customers come flocking in. Heartland serves them with mashed potatoes and creamy gravy, garnished with dried green parsley flakes. It's a flavorful comfort food combo. (If that's not enough, the homemade pies and pastries at Heartland are like your grandma used to make. Coproprietor Maureen Christopher, who owns and operates the business with husband Jim, always has a special "Ooh! Ahh!" dessert to knock your socks off!)

We got the meatball recipe from Charlie, gave it to Ed and Frank, and asked them to try the balls with Ed's sauce and pasta. They added one egg as a binder, wrapped the balls with bacon, smoked them with sauce, and served the concoction on pasta. Everyone raved about it. Now it is one of their favorites when entertaining family and friends in their backyards.

Charlie's Smoked Bacon-Wrapped Meatballs

Serves 6 to 8

Charlie Fenstra, head cook at Heartland, developed this recipe one day when he was messing around in the kitchen trying to come up with an idea for a new special. Since many residents in the Crosby area of Minnesota are of Norwegian and Swedish descent, we're not surprised that Charlie's balls have a slight Scandinavian accent. Although Charlie serves his balls smothered with creamy gravy, we urge you to try them with Ed's BBQ Spaghetti Sauce and pasta this time.

1½ pounds ground beef

1⅓ cups crumbled crackers, such as Keebler Club Crackers

10 ounces fresh white button mushrooms, stems included, minced

1 medium yellow onion, diced

2 large cloves garlic, minced or pressed

1 teaspoon salt

1 teaspoon freshly ground black pepper

1 teaspoon extra virgin olive oil

1 large egg

1 cup shredded Swiss cheese

8 ounces thinly sliced bacon

1 bottle or jar of your favorite barbecue sauce

Preheat the oven to 350°F.

Place the beef in a large bowl. Add the crumbled crackers, mushrooms, onion, garlic, salt, pepper, oil, egg, and cheese. Mix well with your hands.

Form the mixture into balls about 1½ inches in diameter. Put some water in a 9 by 13-inch pan and place the meatballs in the pan. Bake for 20 minutes, or until cooked through.

Heat a smoker to 225°F.

Let the meatballs cool enough to handle, then wrap each ball in one-third of a slice of bacon. Secure the bacon with a toothpick. Put the balls in a 9 by 12-inch aluminum pan (i.e., a half pan), cover with the sauce, and smoke for about 40 minutes, or until the bacon is cooked.

Ed's BBQ Spaghetti Sauce

Makes 1 quart

Frank Kondor (see page 19) suggests you let the sauce rest while you cook about 1 pound of Buitoni pasta until it is just al dente. Add some cooked sausage or meatballs and enjoy.

5 slices bacon, chopped

¾ cup diced yellow onion

¾ cup seeded and diced red bell pepper

2 tablespoons diced jalapeño

1 teaspoon minced garlic

2 tablespoons diced fennel

1 tablespoon minced chipotle
   in adobo sauce

1½ cups ground tomatoes

1½ cups ketchup

¼ cup plus 1 tablespoon apple cider

¼ cup bourbon whiskey
   (Ed uses Old Grand-Dad)

¼ cup Pepsi

2 tablespoons molasses

2 tablespoons cider vinegar

2 tablespoons lemon juice

2 tablespoons spicy brown mustard

2 tablespoons soy sauce

2 tablespoons Worcestershire sauce

3 tablespoons honey

1 teaspoon hot sauce

½ cup firmly packed light brown sugar

½ teaspoon Liquid Smoke

1 teaspoon freshly cracked black pepper

½ teaspoon dried parsley, crushed

½ teaspoon dried basil, crushed

½ teaspoon unsweetened cocoa powder

⅛ teaspoon ground celery seed

⅛ teaspoon ground allspice

Place the bacon in a large pot over medium heat and cook until the fat is rendered. Drain the bacon on paper towels and set it aside.

Add the onion, red bell pepper, and jalapeño to the bacon grease and cook until soft, 2 to 3 minutes. Add the garlic, fennel, and chipotle and cook until soft and fragrant, 2 to 3 minutes.

Add the remaining ingredients and chopped bacon and bring the sauce to a boil. Reduce the heat to a simmer and cook, stirring occasionally, for about 30 minutes. Before serving, run a hand (immersion) blender through the sauce to get a smooth texture.

SPAGHETTI

Happy "Holla" Australian Barbecue Rack of Lamb

Serves 2 to 4

After a long and distinguished career as a barbecue champion, entrepreneur, and active member of the Kansas City Barbeque Society Board of Directors, Ed sold all of his competition barbecue equipment and moved to a small condo. His popular Happy Holla Bar-B-Q Seasoning & Dry Rub is available online and in stores. He has scaled back on cooking barbecue at home. Two of his favorites to cook on his small grill are rack of lamb and pork or chicken quesadillas. Here he shares his secret for a superb grilled rack of lamb with seasonings that complement it perfectly.

3 tablespoons Dijon mustard

1 tablespoon chopped fresh thyme

1 teaspoon ground rosemary

1 teaspoon granulated garlic

Salt and freshly ground black pepper

1 rack of lamb

In a small bowl, mix the mustard, thyme, rosemary, garlic, and salt and pepper to taste to form a paste. Apply it to the meat side of the rack 30 minutes before cooking and let it sit at room temperature while you prepare the grill.

Preheat a grill to medium (see Note).

Place the meat on the grate, cover, and cook for 8 to 10 minutes. Turn and cook for 8 to 10 minutes more, or until the internal temperature registers 125°F for rare and 135°F for medium-rare. Let the meat rest for 10 minutes before carving.

Note: For oven roasting, preheat the oven to 425°F. Sear the rack of lamb in a nonstick pan, meat side down, in 1 tablespoon olive oil for approximately 2 minutes. Place the lamb in a roasting pan and bake for about 20 minutes, or until it reaches your desired doneness (same as for grilling).

ED ROITH, HAPPY HOLLA BBQ TEAM

It all started in 1987. For many years I had enjoyed smoking barbecue, especially ribs, practicing often, achieving what I thought was the perfect product. A friend entered a barbecue contest and asked if I'd like to visit him while competing. His team just happened to win the contest, and I thought I would try entering a contest myself. Over the next 10 years it became a whole new way of life. The barbecue bug bit!

Our team consisted of my late wife, Muriel, and me, and we enjoyed this second life with many accomplishments. We were invited to cook at the Jack Daniel's World Championship nine years straight. Never did win the BIG ONE, but did win many individual places. Over all, we won 375 individual ribbons, plaques, and trophies, as well as 11 state championships, which at that time were only one per state.

I was one of the first 100 members of the Kansas City Barbeque Society, and I served several terms on their board of directors. I also helped initiate their Certified Barbecue Judge and Master Certified Judge program and curriculum.

Pepper Monkey Lamb Meatballs

Makes about 48 meatballs, serving 10 to 12

We had to include this fantastic recipe because the marriage of fresh ginger, garlic, mint, feta cheese, spinach, and freshly ground lamb with complementary spicy seasonings grilled over direct heat yields an outstanding flavor. Cover them with Spicy Afghan Green Sauce and you'll be serving one of the most remarkable backyard barbecues ever. Friends who think they don't like lamb will rave about these meatballs.

SPICY AFGHAN GREEN SAUCE

1 bunch fresh cilantro

½ to 1 jalapeño, depending on how spicy you want your sauce

1 cup loosely packed fresh mint leaves

3 cloves garlic

1 cup plain Greek yogurt

2 tablespoons seasoned salt

Juice of 1 lemon

1 teaspoon agave nectar

MEATBALLS

1 tablespoon cumin seeds (see Notes)

2 tablespoons coriander seeds

Seeds from 4 cardamom pods

Seeds from 2 star anise

1 tablespoon ground turmeric

3 tablespoons seasoned salt

1 tablespoon coarsely ground black pepper

1 teaspoon ground cinnamon

1 teaspoon cayenne

4 to 5 pounds ground lamb (see Notes)

1 medium yellow onion, finely chopped

2 tablespoons peeled, finely chopped fresh ginger

4 cloves garlic, finely chopped

½ bunch fresh mint, chopped

½ cup crumbled feta cheese

1 cup cooked spinach, chopped

Make the Spicy Afghan Green Sauce: Combine all the ingredients in a blender or food processor and puree until smooth. This can be done 1 to 3 days in advance. It is best to make the sauce at least 1 day in advance to give the flavors time to blend.

Preheat a grill to about 375°F for direct cooking.

Make the meatballs: Place the cumin, coriander, cardamom seeds, and star anise in a small skillet over medium heat and toast until fragrant, 2 to 3 minutes. Let cool, then grind in a spice or coffee grinder. Add the turmeric, seasoned salt, black pepper, cinnamon, and cayenne and mix well.

Place the ground lamb in a large bowl. Add the spices along with the onion, ginger, garlic, mint, feta, and spinach and mix well, but do not overmix as this will result in a tough texture. Form the mixture into meatballs 1 to 1½ inches in diameter.

Place the meatballs on the grill grate and cook for about 14 minutes, or until the internal temperature reaches 160°F on a meat thermometer, rotating the meatballs frequently to ensure that they caramelize evenly.

Serve with the dipping sauce.

Notes: You may substitute store-bought garam masala for the homemade spice mixture here.

You can have a butcher grind the meat, or you can do it yourself at home, using a meat grinder or food processor.

JOEL AND ERIN MATTESON, PEPPER MONKEY BBQ

We met in 2004 in the military, the most unfoodie-friendly environment you could imagine. We found creative ways to bypass the standard military Meals Ready to Eat (MRE) and the salt-infused meat by-products, eating off the local economy any chance we got.

That chance encounter was the beginning of a lifetime together. It was a challenge to combine her (Erin's) Pacific Northwest fish-loving tastes with my (Joel's) Midwest better-be-meat-and-potatoes concept of eating. After spending 3 years in the South, we moved to our current home on the East Coast, and our

pantry contains our favorite ingredients and seasonings picked up from living in all regions of the United States. Add this to the fact that we ate food in more than eight different countries during our military adventures, and it is not surprising at all that our dinner table is frequently filled with creations that our families back home may never have dreamt of. All this led to the creation of Pepper Monkey BBQ and a blog where we share our successes and failures in the kitchen in an interactive way that will allow everyone to learn and be able to create dishes right along with us.

Hector Rivera's Charcoalholics Santa Fe Burger with Avocado Mayo and Caramelized Chipotle Onions and Pineapple

Serves 6

Hector developed this recipe for a local burger contest at the urging of a friend. Following his instincts and faith, he penned the recipe on a napkin the night of the competition. He was especially proud of winning first place since he was the only amateur in the contest. Hector later prepared a similar version that won the "I Know Jack About Grilling" contest in 2008 at the Jack Daniel's World Championship Invitational Barbecue. Whether he serves the full-meal burger or his 3.5-ounce Santa Fe sliders in a potato roll, friends love it. The creamy avocado mayo with a complementary balance of spicy and sweet on grilled beef patties will be a winner in your backyard too.

AVOCADO MAYO

1 ripe avocado

1 scallion, white and green parts

1 tablespoon fresh cilantro leaves

Juice of ½ lime

½ cup mayonnaise

CARAMELIZED CHIPOTLE ONIONS AND PINEAPPLE

½ (20-ounce) can crushed pineapple in syrup

¼ cup red wine vinegar

¼ cup sugar

1 tablespoon canola oil

2 medium yellow onions, thinly sliced

1 canned chipotle chile with 1 tablespoon adobo sauce, pureed together

1 tablespoon honey

BURGERS

2 pounds ground sirloin or 88% lean ground beef

1 pound ground pork

3 tablespoons all-purpose seasoning or mixed garlic powder, onion powder, and freshly ground black pepper

¼ cup adobo sauce from canned chipotles

¼ cup Worcestershire sauce

½ cup finely minced yellow onion

Salt and freshly ground black pepper

6 slices mild cheddar cheese

Butter, for the buns

6 hamburger buns

6 leaves red lettuce

6 slices tomato

Make the Avocado Mayo: Slice the avocado in half, discard the pit, and scoop the flesh into a food processor. Add the scallion, cilantro, lime juice, and mayonnaise and pulse until smooth. Transfer to a small bowl, cover, and refrigerate until ready to use.

Make the Caramelized Chipotle Onions and Pineapple: Use a colander to separate the crushed pineapple from the syrup. Reserve ¼ cup of the syrup and save the rest for another use. In a medium saucepan over medium-high heat, combine the red wine vinegar, the syrup from the crushed pineapple, and the sugar. Cook for about 30 minutes to reduce it to a syrupy consistency. Heat the canola oil in a large skillet over medium-low heat. Add the sliced onions and cook for about 45 minutes. Reduce the heat to low, add the pineapple juice reduction, the pureed chipotle, and the honey and cook for another 20 minutes, or until the onions soften and take on a golden color.

Make the burgers: In a large bowl, combine the ground meats, all-purpose seasoning, adobo sauce, Worcestershire, and minced onion and mix well. Form into 6 patties, taking care not to press the meat too hard or pack it together too much. Refrigerate for at least 1 hour before cooking.

Prepare a hot grill. Place the patties on the grate, season with salt and pepper, cover, and cook for 6 to 8 minutes on each side, or until the internal temperature reaches 160°F on a meat thermometer. When the patties are almost done, add a slice of cheese to each and let it melt.

Spread butter on your hamburger buns and toast them on the grill for about 1 minute. Spread each with a little avocado mayo and add caramelized onions, lettuce, and tomato.

HECTOR RIVERA, CHARCOALHOLICS

I have been a certified Charcoalholic since 1996. My interest in barbecue began when I was 16 years old, cooking churrasco for my family in the backyard in Bayamón. In 1996, I entered my first competition, a local Jack Daniel's competition, with some friends and got the smoke bug. I learned a lot about barbecue by reading books. When I went to the 2002 Jack Daniel's World Championship Invitational and won third place in barbecue sauce, I truly learned how to do barbecue right by watching and asking fellow competitors who were very nice and showed me the ropes. I competed for 7 more years at local competitions, and in 2009 I became the head judge for the Cattlemen's BBQ competition. I am also one of the founding fathers of the Caribbean BBQ Association.

Lo'-N-Slo' BBQ's Grilled Stuffed Meat Loaf

Serves 6 to 8

When Chef Paul tested this recipe, we agreed at first bite that it's a crowd-pleaser in the Comfort Food Deluxe genre. Lo'-N-Slo' BBQ's Tom and Michele Perelka (see page 132) gave us the Roasted Garlic Twice-Baked Potatoes (page 140) and Grilled Asparagus (page 132) recipes to go along with their stuffed meat loaf. Your guests will be so full of comfort after this meal that you may want to make it a backyard barbecue and slumber party. Bring your own tent.

1 pound ground chuck

8 ounces ground veal

8 ounces ground pork

2 large eggs

¼ cup milk

Salt and freshly ground black pepper

½ cup breadcrumbs

1 medium yellow onion, diced

¾ cup crumbled feta or other favorite cheese

½ cup sun-dried tomatoes, diced (not packed in oil)

1 roasted red pepper, diced

Fresh basil leaves

Your favorite barbecue sauce, for serving

In a large bowl, combine the beef, veal, and pork. Whisk the eggs and milk together in a separate bowl. Add the egg mixture to the meat mixture and sprinkle in some salt and pepper. Add the breadcrumbs and diced onion. Mix all the ingredients together with a fork, being careful not to overmix.

Place a piece of parchment paper on an 8 by 12-inch tray, making sure the tray is completely covered. Place the meat mixture on the tray and spread out to completely cover the tray in an even layer. Layer the cheese, sun-dried tomatoes, roasted red pepper, and basil over the meat mixture, leaving a ½-inch border around the edges.

Starting on the short side, roll up the meat loaf, peeling back the parchment paper as you roll. Seal up all of the seams and tightly wrap in plastic wrap. Refrigerate for at least 2 hours and up to 6 hours.

Prepare a hot grill (350°F) for indirect cooking. Use a double layer of heavy-duty aluminum foil to create a 16-inch square with 3 slits cut in it. Remove the meat loaf from the plastic wrap and place it on the foil. Place a drip pan on the lower rack. (If you're also making Lo'-N-Slo's potatoes, now would be a good time to roast the garlic and cook the potatoes over indirect heat while you're cooking the meat loaf.)

Cover the grill and cook for 40 minutes. Glaze with barbecue sauce and cook for another 15 to 20 minutes, or until the meat is no longer pink and the internal temperature reaches at least 160°F on a meat thermometer. Let rest for 10 to 15 minutes, then slice with a serrated knife.

Bob Fite's Jiggy Piggy Lamb Racks

Serves 6 to 8

Bob Fite used to have an attitude about lamb. He didn't like it and would even say he hated it. Bob's negative attitude about lamb changed after eating a French-cut lamb chop appetizer prepared by Narvelle Patton, a popular chef and caterer in Huntsville, Alabama. Bob has added his own "Jiggy Piggy" magic to Narvelle's original recipe. He describes it as "a contender in the Friday night 'anything goes' category." He told us Johnny Trigg of the famous Smokin' Triggers barbecue team also thought he hated lamb until he ate these lamb chops.

4 (8-bone) racks French-cut lamb

1 cup firmly packed light brown sugar

1 cup ketchup

1 cup merlot wine

¼ cup soy sauce

1 tablespoon garlic powder

1 tablespoon kosher salt

½ tablespoon freshly ground black pepper

Olive oil spray

Prepare a medium-hot grill.

Remove the membrane from the racks of ribs and separate them into individual bones—this is a fast cook.

Combine the brown sugar, ketchup, wine, soy sauce, garlic powder, salt, and pepper in a large saucepan over medium-low heat and stir until the sugar has dissolved and the mixture is well blended.

Dip the chops in the mixture. Spray the grate with olive oil and lay the dipped chops on the grate. Cover and cook for 3 to 5 minutes. Dip the chops again, turn, cover, and cook for 3 to 5 minutes more for medium rare, or longer, if desired. Serve immediately.

BOB FITE AND STEVE BLAKE, JIGGY PIGGY BBQ

We are co-pitmasters on a pro cooking team from Decatur, Alabama. We've been steady competitors on the southeastern Kansas City Barbeque Society barbecue circuit since 2000. Often accompanied by our wives, Sherry and Claudia, Jiggy Piggy has won more than a dozen Grand Championships and is the current Alabama BBQ Trail and the American Bass Anglers' 2009 Champion.

Jaan's Barbecue Meat "Cake"

Serves 10 to 12

Jaan's barbecue meat cake is as memorable as it is tasty. What could be better and more appropriate for the backyard birthday celebration of a barbecue friend? It looks like a dessert, but as Jaan tells us, it's really "a history-making meat wreath." He has entered it in several competitions under "home cooking from the homeland" and similar categories. This illusory food draws inspiration from culinary customs in the Hansa Union towns of Europe during the Middle Ages. Dishes were customarily made to look like well-known food, but created from ingredients completely different from what one would expect.

6 (1- to 1½-pound) pork tenderloins

4 ounces (about ¾ cup) golden raisins

4 ounces (about 1 cup) walnuts, minced

1 cup of your favorite spicy barbecue rub

4 ounces unsweetened chocolate, finely grated

Preheat a smoker to 220°F. Spray a 9-inch round cake pan with nonstick cooking spray.

Using a long, sharp knife, trim the silver skin and fat from the tenderloins. Starting about 1½ inches in from the thickest end (leaving the very end uncut), insert the knife and cut each tenderloin into three equal layers (each approximately ½ inch thick) down through the tail. Each tenderloin should remain in one piece at the thickest end. Set aside about ¼ cup each of the raisins and walnuts. Combine the remaining raisins and walnuts with the rub and massage the mixture onto the tenderloins.

Place the tenderloins in the prepared cake pan, evenly spaced, with the blunt, thick ends pressed against the sides of the pan and the tapered, layered ends pointing toward the middle of the pan. Twist or weave together the layers of each tenderloin and arrange them in a spiral shape around the middle of the pan. All together, the tenderloins should now be in the shape of a wreath. Sprinkle the reserved raisins and nuts over the top. Cover the meat "cake" with foil.

Place in the smoker, cover, and cook for about 1½ hours, or until the internal temperature reaches between 140°F (for medium rare) and 165°F (for well done) on a meat thermometer. Remove the pan from the smoker, uncover it, and let it rest for 10 to 15 minutes.

The "meat" cake looks delicious without the chocolate finish, but the finish adds a special touch. Invert the cake pan onto a serving platter. Sprinkle the grated chocolate over the still-hot meat, let it melt a little, then use a spatula to spread it evenly over the meat. Slice and serve.

JAAN HABICHT, PARK GOURMET BBQ TEAM

Jaan Habicht, the "Grandfather of Estonian Barbecue" and "Russian Barbecue King," had a barbecue epiphany at a world barbecue championship in Lisdoonvarna, Ireland, in 1989. Besides Jaan, the Estonian team included some of the best restaurant chefs from Estonia and Ene Ojaveski, a rising Estonian culinary star. This was the first time Jaan and the team had competed in a barbecue contest. Team Estonia met Team Kansas City. Call it karma or Irish luck, but both teams benefited. Chef Paul Kirk, Chef Ronaldo Camargo, Chef Karen Putnam, and the KC Rib Doctor, Guy Simpson, mentored the Estonian team. In return, Team Estonia introduced Team Kansas City to European-style culinary competition. Team Kansas City won the world championship that year and went on to become Grand Champion at the new Jack Daniel's World Championship Invitational Barbecue. Jaan and several teammates were inspired to compete at the Memphis in May Barbecue and the American Royal Invitational in Kansas City and elsewhere in the United States. Jaan is a founding father of the Estonian National Barbecue Association. He is one of the organizers of the Estonian Grillfest and hosted the Barbecue Fish 2012 contest at the Golden Fish celebration in Viljandi, Estonia.

Bob Lyon's Chicken Wing Sections

Serves 6 to 8

Bob's favorite barbecue morsel is the second bone of the chicken wing, but since the second bone is usually sold attached to the drumettes, he usually barbecues them as one piece. Using the method below, it takes about 1 hour and 15 minutes to barbecue two dozen pieces. These bones are so popular at backyard gatherings that Bob, of the Beaver Castors team (see page 111), always plans on grilling a second or third batch. Bob often hears satisfied guests say, "That's the best piece of barbecue I've had all day!"

MUSTARD SLATHER

2 cups prepared mustard

½ cup dill pickle juice

2 tablespoons Worcestershire sauce

1 tablespoon hot pepper sauce

JALAPEÑO-GARLIC GLAZE

2 tablespoons jarred crushed garlic

1 cup green jalapeño jelly

1 cup apple juice

CHICKEN WINGS

2 dozen chicken wings, tips removed

¼ cup of your favorite barbecue rub

Make the Mustard Slather: Combine all the ingredients in a small bowl and blend well. Set aside.

Make the Jalapeño-Garlic Glaze: Combine all the ingredients in a small saucepan and bring to a boil over medium-high heat. Reduce the heat and simmer, stirring with a wire whisk, until the mixture is reduced by half. Set aside.

Prepare a medium grill. Bob likes to use charcoal and a small chunk of hickory or wild cherry wood for smoke.

Brush both sides of the wings with the mustard slather and sprinkle with the rub. Place the wings on the grate close to but not directly over the heat, meat side down. Cover and cook for 50 minutes. Brush with glaze, turn, and cook until done, about 10 minutes.

FunSeakers Dixie Pixie Wings

Serves 4 to 6

When Dixie met Pixie one sunny day in Key West, sparks flew, and free-range chickens scattered! Patty Adams did the prep work. "That was easy," she exclaimed, as she handed the marinated chicken wings to Mike after he dumped a chimney full of hot charcoal briquettes into his grill, sprayed the grate with canola, and grabbed his long-handled tongs. That's when the sparks flew. "As soon as you've grilled them to perfection, I'll sprinkle some Pixie Dust on them," said Patty. Thus began the makings of a perfect feast that was so good it is oft repeated. This recipe is so easy and so delicious you won't believe it. DennyMike's Carolina-style sauce is the "Dixie" in this story; his Pixie Dust is Pixie. Here is the FunSeakers basic recipe for a chicken wing feast on the beach or in your backyard.

3 pounds chicken wings, disjointed and tips removed

2 cups Carolina barbecue sauce, preferably DennyMike's Carolina-Style BahBQue & Slathah Sauce, plus more for serving

½ cup DennyMike's Pixie Dust or your favorite rub

Place the wings in a zipper bag, pour in the barbecue sauce, and marinate in the refrigerator for at least 2 hours and up to overnight.

Prepare a medium-hot grill.

Remove the wings from the marinade and dispose of the marinade. Grill the wings over the hot coals, turning every 2 to 3 minutes until done, 10 to 12 minutes. When the wings are done, transfer them to a serving dish, sprinkle with the rub, and serve with the sauce on the side.

PATTY AND MIKE ADAMS, FUNSEAKERS COMPETITION BBQ TEAM

We—Mike, a California boy (read: Left Coast), and Patty, a Portland, Maine, girl (Right Coast)—made our careers in the insurance business in Portland, Maine, for 25-plus years before grabbing the brass ring and retiring to the fabulous Florida Keys and, more specifically, Sugarloaf Key. In paradise, it became quite a habit to head down loaded for bear with lobsters and BBQ, as well as a small store of adult beverages, lest one become parched from the hot sun. Some three or four years ago our good friend DennyMike Sherman, who owns a barbecue business, brought us a nice little pellet smoker. Mike got handy with the smoker, and now we've got the whole of Sugarloaf Key smoking! It's turned into one big party, with Yankees bringing outrageously tasty barbecue, uniquely prepared, using another Yankee's sauces and rubs, down south, where barbecue got its beginnings.

Big Billy's BBQ Sticky Lemon-Pepper Chicken Wings

Serves 6 to 8

Summertime family gatherings have created some fond memories for barbecue maestro Billy Rodgers. It is the smell of charcoal being lit and the sound of music playing in harmony to the hum of friends and family telling tall tales with fun-loving endings! His father, Willie Frank, an excellent cook, enjoys reminding Billy about a visit to a maternal grandmother's house one summer. His mother had bought a new cast-iron grill and began inviting family and friends to a cookout. (His dad knew better than to fire the grill up without seasoning it first, right?) According to Billy's dad, either the grill thermometer or the drink of the day confirmed that the grill was hot and ready, so he threw on some chicken pieces. While he was cooking, he alleges that Billy paid several visits to make sure things were being cooked properly. Whether it was the pressure of that supervision or the drink of the day, the chicken was burned more than new wood being made into lump charcoal! Billy supposedly swore he wouldn't eat it, but later, after several inspections, he did eat a hot dog.

If you don't burn these wings, you and your guests will savor the marriage of sweet and spicy citrus accents that complement the crispy magic imparted from the grill. There's a lot of flavor going on with these wings, and it all adds up to delicious. Billy dedicates this recipe to his Dad and his "secret" ingredient—lemon!

MARINADE

½ cup clover honey

½ cup plus 2 tablespoons lemon juice

3 tablespoons thinly sliced scallion, white and green parts

2 tablespoons peeled, grated fresh ginger

6 cloves garlic, crushed

½ teaspoon five-spice powder

¼ cup tamari sauce or soy sauce

⅔ cup lemon curd or lemon marmalade

½ cup hot sesame oil

2 teaspoons salt

4 teaspoons coarsely ground black pepper

2 teaspoons hot red pepper flakes (optional)

CHICKEN WINGS

12 large chicken wings, cut into segments and tips removed

Mix together all of the marinade ingredients in a small bowl. Place the chicken wing segments and marinade together in a gallon-size zipper freezer bag. Seal tightly and refrigerate overnight.

Preheat a grill to 350°F for direct cooking. After 15 minutes, take a wire brush and clean your grill grates. Using a pair of tongs, dip a folded paper towel or a piece of cheesecloth into a small bowl of vegetable oil. Rub the oiled paper towel/cheesecloth on the grill grates to help create a nonstick cooking surface.

Carefully remove the wing segments from the marinade, shaking the excess liquid from the wings back into the bag. Discard the leftover marinade.

Place the wing segments on the grate. Cover and cook for 10 minutes. Turn and continue to cook until the internal temperature reaches 180°F and the juices run clear, 10 to 15 minutes longer.

BILLY RODGERS, BIG BILLY'S BBQ

I began my quest for barbecue excellence in 2003 by taking my first class from chef Paul Kirk. I continued honing my skills by assisting Paul in various contests, as well as organizing various barbecue classes for Paul and a Kansas City Barbeque Society class for new judges.

I competed in my first solo contest, the Great American Barbecue contest held in Kansas City, in 2007. My proudest achievement is winning the Diddy-Wa-Diddy National Barbecue Sauce Contest sponsored by the Great American Barbecue contest in 2010. The highlight of winning the contest was personally receiving my award from Ardie Davis aka Remus Powers!

Harry Soo's Slapilicious Buttermilk Fried Chicken

Serves 2 to 4

The first several years we competed in or judged at the Memphis in May World Championship Barbecue Cooking Contest, the adventure wasn't complete without a side trip to Mason, Tennessee, for a pulled pork sandwich at Bozo's and fried chicken at Gus's. Lately we've switched to barbecue spaghetti at the Bar-B-Q Shop in Memphis and fried chicken at the new Gus's in downtown Memphis. The last time we were at Gus's in Mason we tried to get the fried chicken recipe from Taurus, Gus's son. He wouldn't turn loose of a single ingredient. We suspect, however, that buttermilk, flour, and cayenne pepper were involved. Harry Soo adds some barbecue rub to the mix for a flavor signature that rivals any other fried chicken we've ever had, except what our mothers fried for Sunday after-church lunch! Chef Paul has added some enhancements to Harry's online recipe. We hope you're as pleased as we are with the result.

1 small (3- to 3½-pound) whole chicken

Slap Yo' Daddy (SYD) Competition Meat Rub or your favorite rub (see Note)

Cayenne (optional)

2 cups all-purpose flour

2 tablespoons yellow cornmeal

1 tablespoon baking powder

2 cups buttermilk

4 cups pork lard or oil of choice

Cut the chicken into 12 pieces (or ask your butcher to do it). First, remove the backbone and wing tips and reserve for another use. Cut the chicken in half, remove the wings, and cut in half. Cut the thigh and leg off and cut the breast in half. Repeat with the other half and you should have 12 pieces.

Place the chicken in a small baking dish and season all over with rub. Sprinkle with cayenne if desired. Cover and refrigerate for at least 1 hour, or longer if desired.

Combine the flour, cornmeal, 2 tablespoons of the rub, and the baking powder in a shallow dish and blend well. Set aside.

Drain the chicken in a colander for 10 minutes. Dredge the chicken in the flour mixture. Let rest on a wire rack for 10 minutes. Dip the chicken in the buttermilk, then dredge it in the flour mixture again, shaking off the excess flour.

Preheat a cast-iron skillet with 4 cups lard until it registers 360°F on a deep-frying thermometer. Fry the chicken in small batches, starting with the thighs, legs, and breast and taking care not to crowd the chicken. When the bottoms are brown, turn the chicken pieces over. The pieces should be done in 7 to 15 minutes, depending on the size of the pieces and the quantity you have in the pan. The chicken is done when the juices run clear when pierced with the tip of a knife. Use an instant-read thermometer to ensure that the meat at the center is more than 165°F. Repeat for the remaining pieces.

Drain the chicken thoroughly on paper towels, sprinkle with some finishing rub, if desired, and serve immediately.

Note: To make your own rub, combine 1 tablespoon sea salt, 2 teaspoons finely ground black pepper, 1 teaspoon granulated garlic, 1 teaspoon sugar, and ½ teaspoon mild chili powder and blend well.

HARRY SOO, SLAP YO' DADDY

In 2008, Slap Yo' Daddy was recognized in our first year out as California's Rookie Team of the Year. Team Slap Yo' Daddy went on to rack up impressive recognition as Arizona and California Team of the Year in 2010, plus third place overall in America with its Kansas City Barbeque Society ranking. The team earned instant fame in the competition barbecue network and made appearances on TV shows and other media. Slap Yo' Daddy is winning more contests and growing its fan base. At last count we have won more than two dozen grand championships. Our dynamic personality, team spirit, generosity, and disciplined attention to details have won us the respect and friendship of everyone we meet on the barbecue trail.

Bill Minahan's Classic Red Sauce

Serves 6 to 8

This recipe honors Bill's hometown roots in the Italian district of Boston, known as the North End. His recipe marries centuries-old Italian flavor profiles with the flavor of real barbecue.

He calls it an Italian/barbecue fusion. We call it a culinary masterpiece! You can serve it over pasta or use it in Bill's chicken and prosciutto fatties (page 106).

2 tablespoons olive oil

½ medium sweet onion, chopped

1 tablespoon chopped garlic

1 (6-ounce) can tomato paste

1 (12-ounce) can ground peeled tomatoes

1½ cups water

1 tablespoon chopped fresh basil

½ teaspoon salt

½ teaspoon freshly ground black pepper

½ teaspoon chopped fresh oregano

¼ teaspoon Tabasco sauce

Place the olive oil in a large pot over medium heat. Add the onion and cook for 3 to 5 minutes or until browned. Add the garlic and cook for 2 minutes, stirring constantly and being careful not to burn it. Add the tomato paste and cook for 3 to 5 minutes, or until caramelized, stirring constantly. Add the tomatoes and water. Stir. Add the basil, garlic, salt, pepper, oregano, and Tabasco and bring to a boil. Reduce the heat and simmer for 3 hours.

Bill Minahan's New York Strip with Alaskan King Crab and Shrimp

Serves 4

Bill Minahan's passion for cooking began with learning to cook Italian favorites—only natural for someone growing up in Boston's North End. When he got hooked on barbecue, Bill (see page 104) held on to his Italian flavor profiles and fused them with his barbecue expertise. The results continue to please his family, friends, and fellow pitmasters on the barbecue circuit, present company included. This steak, crab, and shrimp masterpiece is rich on flavor and sure to please the special guests you invite to the party.

24 medium shrimp

½ Alaskan king crab (legs only)

2 (12-ounce) New York strip steaks

2 tablespoons olive oil

1 teaspoon salt

1 teaspoon coarsely ground black pepper

1 tablespoon chopped garlic

2 cups dry sherry or your favorite white wine

8 tablespoons (1 stick) butter

½ lemon

½ cup clam or chicken broth

1 tablespoon chopped fresh parsley

Preheat a grill to 500°F.

Peel and devein the shrimp. Cut the crab legs open for easier eating. Set aside.

Rub the steaks with 1 tablespoon of the olive oil, the salt, and pepper. Place the steaks on the grate, cover, and cook to the desired doneness. Bill cooks them for about 2 minutes, rotates for grilling marks, cooks for another 2 minutes, flips the steaks, cooks for 2 minutes more, rotates again for grilling marks, and finishes them for 2 minutes for a total cooking time of 8 minutes. Let the steaks rest while you cook the crab and shrimp.

Reduce the grill temperature to 400°F. Place the crab legs on the grate, cover, and cook for 10 minutes.

Meanwhile, in a medium pan over medium heat, heat the remaining 1 tablespoon olive oil for about 5 minutes. Add the shrimp and cook for about 3 minutes, or until the shrimp begin to turn pink. Add the garlic and cook for about 2 minutes, stirring constantly and being careful not to let it burn. Add the sherry and cook for 2 minutes. Add the butter, squeeze the lemon juice into the pan, then place the lemon face down in the sauce and cook for 3 minutes.

Add the broth, parsley, and the crab legs from the grill and cook for 3 minutes. Serve immediately with the sliced steaks.

Bill Minahan's Chicken and Prosciutto Fatties

Makes 2 fatties, serving 8 to 10

What's the difference between a fatty—also known as phatties—and meat loaf? One is a combination of ground meats mixed with a variety of tasty ingredients and cooked until done. The other is what happens if you eat too much! Seriously, we won't argue with you if you want to call your fatty a glorified meat loaf. Bubba Bill's rendition, with a distinctly Italian palate-pleasing accent, is a true classic. Please make sure you smoke it—and call us when it's ready.

1 ½ to 2 pounds bulk sweet Italian sausage

8 ounces ricotta cheese

2 boneless, skinless chicken breasts, chopped

2 tablespoons chopped fresh basil

1 (8-ounce) ball buffalo mozzarella cheese, cut into small cubes

8 ounces Taleggio sharp Italian cheese, cut into small cubes

4 ounces prosciutto

1 recipe Bill Minahan's Classic Red Sauce (page 104)

2 tablespoons freshly grated Parmigiano-Reggiano

Chopped fresh parsley, for garnish

Heat a smoker to 275°F.

Place a sheet of wax paper on your work surface and roll the sausage into a large rectangle about ¼ inch thick on it. Split the rectangle into 2 equal halves.

Spread half the ricotta cheese on each sausage rectangle, leaving a ½-inch perimeter uncovered. Add the chopped chicken and basil. Add the mozzarella and Taleggio cheeses. Cover each with prosciutto.

Using the wax paper, slowly roll each sausage into a long roll. Pinch together the seams and the ends. Apply a light coating of red sauce to the bottom of an 8 by 10-inch baking pan. Place the sausage rolls in the pan and place the pan in the smoker. When cooking Bill likes to add a little apple wood smoke. After 45 minutes, use the remaining red sauce to cover the fatties. You may need to add 3 to 6 ounces of water to the pan if the sauce begins to burn. Cook for an additional 45 minutes.

Allow the meat to rest for 10 minutes. Cut into ¼-inch slices and sprinkle each with a little Parmigiano-Reggiano and parsley.

BILL MINAHAN, QUE AND A HALF MEN

I got involved in competition barbecue in 2009 through fellow members of the Fraternal Order of the Eagles 841, Rockland, Massachusetts, and the Smoke Off held every September. At that time, the club had two traveling teams: Mad Mike's Smokin' Hawgs Competition BBQ Team and Birds of a Feather BBQ Team. Through volunteer cooking and the passion I had shown for the Eagles events, I was invited to cook with the Smokin' Hawgs. Before I joined the team, it had marginal success. Through my efforts, the team began to realize some success by building processes and consistent product, and we were able to measure the success or failure of a recipe. The Birds of a Feather courted me and made me an offer I could not refuse: pit boss.

For the remaining three events of 2011, Birds of a Feather had the opportunity to move the team scores considerably higher than what was previously achieved, finishing with a team-high 625 points at the Harvard Fall Festival in Harvard, Massachusetts. I also had the opportunity to cook with the Smokin' Hawgs Competition BBQ from Abington, Massachusetts, at the 2011 American Royal Invitational and judge the 2011 American Royal Open. They went on to become the Grand Champion of the Jack Daniel's a few weeks later, and I was able to spend a bit of time socializing with the barbecue greats.

Dizzy Pig Tsunami Duck Breast

Serves 4

Chris Capell calls these duck breasts "a carnival in your mouth." Chris's directions are easy to follow; you just have to be attentive. In addition to being flavorful, duck is fattier than chicken. Count on flare-ups and move the meat to a cool zone periodically to let the fat burn off and to avoid burning the meat. Since Dizzy Pig Tsunami Spin has distinctly Asian flavors, we recommend the Dizzy Pig blend, or you can develop your own Asian dry rub recipe with seasonings such as powdered ginger, cinnamon, anise, brown sugar, black pepper, salt, and granulated garlic. Chris says you won't need sauce with these breasts since so much is going on with the melding of duck meat, duck fat, and seasonings. If you must sauce the breasts, Chris recommends a sweet and spicy sauce with ginger. With or without sauce, we hope your mouth enjoys this carnival as much as ours did!

4 boneless, skin-on duck breasts

**Dizzy Pig Tsunami Spin seasoning,
  or your favorite rub**

Preheat a hot grill.

Rinse the meat under cold water and pat dry. With a sharp knife, score the skin diagonally, leaving ½ inch between cuts, then repeat perpendicular to your first cuts. Try not to cut all the way through to the meat, but only through the outer layer of skin to the fat.

Apply the seasoning generously on the meat side and set aside for 5 to 10 minutes. Flip skin side up and apply a lighter coat of rub on the skin.

Lightly oil the grate. Place the duck breasts on the grate skin down over the high heat, cover, and cook until well browned and sizzling, 4 to 5 minutes. An extended flare-up can easily burn your duck, so watch closely and either cut off the air or keep moving the duck out of the flames. Cooking in small batches of 1 to 2 pieces will also help you control the browning process without flare-ups.

Turn meat side down, cover, reduce the heat to medium-hot, and cook until the internal temperature reaches 130°F. Rest for 5 minutes, under loosely tented foil. Slice thinly across the grain and prepare for a carnival on your taste buds.

CHRIS CAPELL, DIZZY PIG

My infatuation with flavors began when my college buddies had a beer and ale tasting event in 1983. A few years later I married my Vietnamese wife. Her family used ingredients I had never been exposed to, and their technique was beautiful. The balance of flavors, browning of the food, and intense preparation techniques were inspiring. Their use of ginger, lemongrass, fresh garlic, various other exotic herbs and the all-powerful fish sauce totally blew my mind. Their use of a super-hot wok also opened my eyes as to how much high heat can enhance flavor.

About 15 years ago I purchased my first charcoal cooker, a Big Green Egg, and began a quest to combine my well-developed palate, my creative background, and fire and smoke to create food that would hopefully be

the best my guests had ever eaten. I left my design career a few years later to build the Dizzy Pig BBQ Company. We've created many unique spice blends. We got into competition barbecue because we wanted to see how our seasonings would do in a blind judging situation. Since most people are taught to always say the food they are offered is good (which often means lying), we wanted to see what certified judges would think if we used only Dizzy Pig rubs, straight from the bottle.

Our team started competing in 2002 and has competed in nearly 100 contests. I took my team to the American Royal Invitational and the Jack Daniel's World Championship Invitational for 6 years straight, and the last year we were invited (2009), we placed top 10 overall in both prestigious contests.

Bob Lyon's Grand Gaucho Paella

Serves 8 to 10

Bob developed this recipe in response to his wife Sandra's challenge to grill instead of smoke the meat and shellfish for his birthday party paella. He credits Sandra for having a hand in making it over-the-top delicious. They adapted it from Julee Rosso and Sheila Lukin's *New Basics Cookbook*, replacing some of the meats and other ingredients to suit their own taste. The first bite and each bite thereafter is a party in your mouth. Happy birthday, Bob. Any day and any time your paella is ready, give us a call!

CHICKEN

½ cup dry red wine

¼ cup olive oil

2 cloves garlic, minced (or more, if you like)

Grated zest of ½ orange

½ teaspoon salt

Freshly ground black pepper

About 2½ pounds chicken thighs or wings

SHRIMP

¼ cup olive oil

2 cloves garlic, minced (or more, if you like)

1 tablespoon chopped fresh rosemary leaves

½ teaspoon hot red pepper flakes

12 jumbo shrimp in their shells

SAFFRON RICE

¼ cup olive oil

1 medium red onion, coarsely chopped

1 red bell pepper, cored, seeded, and coarsely chopped

1 green bell pepper, cored, seeded, and coarsely chopped

1 yellow or orange bell pepper, cored, seeded, and coarsely chopped

6 cloves garlic, minced

4 cups long-grain white rice

8 cups chicken stock or canned broth

1½ teaspoons saffron threads

1 cup small green Spanish olives

1 cup imported black olives

12 to 16 cherrystone or other small clams, well scrubbed

1 pound mussels, well scrubbed and bearded just before cooking

1 pound garlic or hot Italian sausage, in 1 piece or cut into serving-size pieces

1½ tablespoons olive oil

At least ½ cup chopped fresh cilantro, for garnish

Prepare the chicken: In a dish wide enough to marinate the chicken, combine the wine, olive oil, garlic, orange zest, salt, and pepper and stir well. Add the chicken, cover, and refrigerate overnight, turning once or twice.

Prepare the shrimp: In another shallow dish, combine the olive oil, garlic, rosemary, and red pepper flakes and stir well. Add the shrimp, cover, and refrigerate for several hours.

About 1 hour before serving, prepare the rice: Heat the oil in a large saucepan over medium heat and sauté the onion, peppers, and garlic for 10 minutes. Stir in the rice and cook until translucent, about 5 minutes. Add the stock and saffron and bring to a boil. Lower the heat and simmer, uncovered, until the rice is just tender, about 18 minutes. Stir in the olives and transfer the rice to a large paella pan or an ovenproof platter. Keep it warm in a 250°F oven or on the edge of the grill if it is large enough.

Prepare a hot grill for direct cooking.

Remove the chicken from the marinade and grill over high heat, turning 4 to 5 times, for 10 to 20 minutes, until done to your taste. Add the cooked chicken to the rice or keep it warm on the back of the grill or in the warm oven.

Remove the shrimp from the marinade and grill over high heat for about 2 minutes on each side, or less for smaller shrimp. Add the shrimp to the rice to keep warm.

Arrange the clams and mussels in one layer on the grill and cook until just opened, 8 to 10 minutes. Add them to the rice.

Skewer a long sausage into a spiral (or place smaller pieces on the grill), brush with olive oil, and grill over high heat until lightly charred and cooked through, about 7 minutes per side.

Arrange the sausage and other ingredients decoratively over the rice. Sprinkle the whole dish with lots of cilantro and serve.

BOB LYON, BEAVER CASTORS BBQ TEAM

The Beaver Castors were called the "Road Team of the 90s" by the National Barbecue News. We competed in the first American Royal and Jack Daniel's invitationals in '88 and '89, continuing an unbroken string in both for 10 years—the only team in the country to do so. The high point was reserve championships at both events in 1993. We also competed in the first North Carolina and Tennessee State Championships under Kansas City Barbeque Society scoring systems, winning the former in 1994, a week after winning the Oregon Championship, and the latter in 1995. Another 10-year string took place in Terlingua, Texas, with 6 top 6 places between 1991 and 2000 with firsts in 1996 and 2000 at what became the Bob Roberts Memorial Brisket Championship. Along with three more trips each to North Carolina and Tennessee, we also made Bad Byron's Florida Panhandle event and a BarbeQlossal in Des Moines, Iowa. Since we were coming from Seattle, friends Tony Stone and Steve Holbrook provided the equipment, fuel, and most meat. The team includes me, Jim Erickson, Dave Annon, Derek Maida, and later additions George King and Bill Seewer. Since 2000, we have made several more trips to the American Royal Open and the first Great American Barbecue.

KCass Ahi Tuna Topped with Mango Salsa

Serves 2

When you're looking for backyard fare that is low on prep time and high on flavor, this recipe from Rich and Bunny Tuttle of KCass BBQ is it. It is perfect for any occasion, but especially when your party features a tropical theme.

MANGO SALSA

1 mango, peeled, pitted, and chopped

½ medium red onion, minced

1 whole habanero pepper, minced

1 teaspoon lime juice

TUNA

2 ahi tuna steaks, 1 inch thick

Sesame oil to coat the steaks

Red leaf lettuce, for serving

1 yellow bell pepper, cored, seeded, and thinly sliced

1 medium ripe tomato, cut into wedges

Garlic bread, for serving

Prepare a medium-hot grill.

Make the Mango Salsa: Combine all the ingredients in a small bowl and toss to coat. Set aside.

Coat the tuna steaks on both sides with the sesame oil. Place the steaks on the grate, cover, and cook until medium-rare, 3 to 4 minutes per side.

Place the steaks on a bed of lettuce and top with the Mango Salsa. Arrange slices of fresh yellow peppers and tomato wedges around the fish and serve with garlic toast.

Key West Fintastic Garlic Shrimp

Serves 6 to 10

When Canadians Ron and Bonnie Coffin (see page 77) met Mainer DennyMike Sherman on a fishing expedition in the Florida Keys a few winters ago, the barbecue bug started biting. That's what happens when you're around DennyMike. Winters in their Sugarloaf Key beach hut are frequently highlighted by these fantastic grilled garlic shrimp. This is a memorable dish to serve your guests any time of year and in any locale. The secret is in the right mix of seasonings and a perfect grill time. Served over rice as an entrée, these shrimp are beyond delicious!

1½ to 3½ pounds (27 to 63) cooked large shrimp, peeled and deveined

1 cup olive oil

1 tablespoon DennyMike's Fintastic Savory Seafood Seasoning or your favorite seafood seasoning

1 tablespoon minced garlic

1 teaspoon garlic powder

Garlic butter, for brushing

1 lemon

Place all the ingredients in a gallon-size zipper bag and seal tightly. Gently turn to mix everything. Refrigerate for several hours. Meanwhile, soak some wooden skewers in water.

Preheat a grill to medium.

Thread the shrimp onto the skewers. Place the skewers onto the grate and cook just long enough to warm them, basting often with garlic butter and squeezing fresh lemon juice over them. Serve immediately.

Bill Gillespie's Shrimp Tacos

Makes 8 tacos

Fish tacos—especially with panko-crusted tilapia—are the rage these days. When you serve Bill's shrimp tacos at your next backyard barbecue your guests will add shrimp tacos to their taco favorites. Bill's combo of cool, refreshing sour cream, mayo, lime, and coleslaw, kissed with a lip-tingling touch of jalapeño and cilantro, marries perfectly with the grilled shrimp.

SLAW

¼ cup sour cream

2 tablespoons mayonnaise

Grated zest and juice of 1 lime

1 (16-ounce) package coleslaw mix

2 scallions, white and green parts, diced

1 jalapeño, seeded and diced

2 tablespoons chopped fresh cilantro

Salt and freshly ground black pepper

1 large tomato, seeded and diced

SHRIMP

About 24 (1 pound) uncooked shrimp, peeled and deveined

½ cup canola oil

Salt and freshly ground black pepper

¼ to ½ cup of your favorite seafood seasoning (Smokin' Hoggz uses their own blend)

1 to 1½ cups Thai sweet chili sauce, for serving

8 (6-inch) corn tortillas (flour tortillas are okay)

Make the slaw: In a large bowl, combine the sour cream, mayonnaise, half of the lime zest, and all of the lime juice. Add the coleslaw mix, scallions, jalapeño, and cilantro and mix well. Season with salt and pepper. Stir in the tomato. Refrigerate for about 2 hours or up to 24 hours.

Make the shrimp: Prepare a hot grill for direct cooking.

In a large bowl, toss the shrimp with the canola oil, the remaining lime zest, and some salt and pepper and let sit for about 30 minutes. If using wooden skewers, soak them in water while the shrimp marinate.

Thread the shrimp on the skewers, then season with your favorite rub. Grill directly over the coals for 2 to 3 minutes per side. Remove the shrimp from the grill and from the skewers and toss them in the sweet chili sauce.

Place the tortillas on the grill grate to heat for about 1 minute per side.

To assemble the tacos, spoon some slaw into the bottom of each tortilla, top with 3 shrimp, and enjoy!

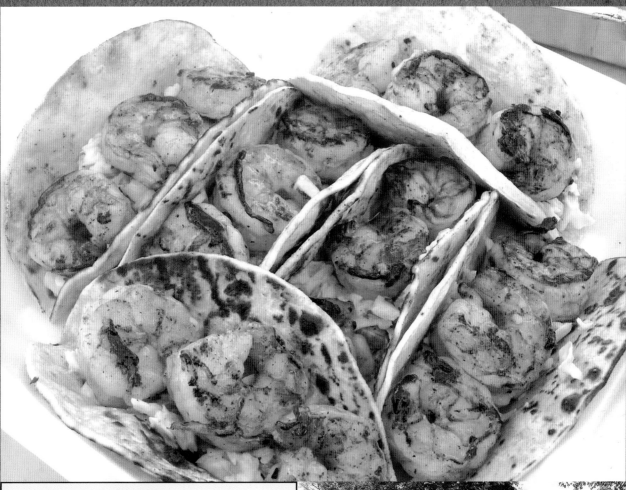

BILL GILLESPIE, SMOKIN' HOGGZ

I got involved in competition barbecue because I love food—especially barbecue and, more specifically, ribs. Before I started competing I had a small little Brinkmann Gourmet charcoal smoker, and almost every weekend I would get together with friends and family and cook all kinds of barbecue on the Brinkmann, trying to hone my skills. One day, a couple of guys I worked with invited me to a barbecue competition, and they let me cook for the "anything butt" category. I got fourth place, and I've been hooked ever since.

Scottie Johnson's Shrimp-Stuffed Avocados with Citrus Aioli

Serves 2 to 4

Scottie Johnson (see page 129), like all great barbecue champions, can play by the rules when the rules are in play. Put him in the backyard, where the only rule is "Give us something delicious!" and his creativity runs rampant! What better proof than these shrimp-stuffed avocados? Scottie serves this with Roasted Pesto Corn Salad (page 129).

CITRUS AIOLI

¼ cup light mayonnaise

4 teaspoons freshly squeezed orange juice

2 teaspoons minced fresh garlic

1 teaspoon grated orange zest

1 teaspoon grated lime zest

Kosher salt

Cayenne

SHRIMP

3 tablespoons extra virgin olive oil

1 tablespoon chopped fresh parsley

1 tablespoon freshly squeezed lime juice

½ teaspoon garlic powder

½ teaspoon hot red pepper flakes

12 ounces shrimp, peeled and deveined

2 medium-firm avocados, halved and pitted

Juice of ½ lime

1 (½-inch-thick) slice red onion

⅓ cup halved grape tomatoes

Preheat a grill to medium-high heat.

Make the aioli: Combine the mayonnaise, orange juice, garlic, zests, salt, and cayenne to taste in a small bowl. Mix well, cover, and refrigerate.

Make the shrimp: Mix 2 tablespoons of the olive oil with the parsley, lime juice, garlic powder, and red pepper flakes in a medium bowl; add the shrimp and toss to coat.

Brush the avocado halves with the remaining 1 tablespoon of olive oil and the juice of ½ lime. Place the shrimp, avocados (flesh side down), and onion over direct heat, uncovered. Grill the shrimp until pink, 3 to 5 minutes. Grill the avocados until bright green and grill marks appear, about 5 minutes. Grill the red onion until softened, about 5 minutes.

Remove from the grill. Scoop out and dice the top two-thirds of flesh from each avocado, leaving the bottom third in the shell. Dice the grilled onion. Gently stir the diced avocado, onion, shrimp, and tomatoes together in a bowl. Spoon the mixture into the avocado shells. Drizzle some aioli over each serving.

Rick Naug's Pacific Northwest Razor Clams

Serves 6 as an appetizer or 4 as a main course

Rick Naug uses razor clams due to their sweet taste and delicate texture. If razor clams are not available in your area, you can order them online. You can also use littleneck, Manila, or any other fresh clams available from your favorite fishmonger. Be sure to discard all clams that have broken or open shells. For best results, cook these clams hot and fast. With a cast-iron skillet, a hot grill, and a few simple ingredients, you can cook up a backyard appetizer or entrée that your guests will love—even those who thought they didn't like seafood.

8 tablespoons (1 stick) salted butter

¼ cup white wine (Riesling, chardonnay, or your favorite)

1 pound razor clams, rinsed

Saltine crackers and lemon wedges, for serving

Finely chopped fresh parsley, for garnish

Finely chopped scallions, white and green parts, for garnish

Heat the butter in a cast-iron skillet over high heat until just melted. Add the wine and continue heating for about 30 seconds. Add the clams and cook for 3 to 5 minutes, or until the clam shells begin to open and the meat starts to curl at the edges and forms a broth. Be careful not to overcook. Overcooked clams will be leathery and tasteless.

Serve the clams and broth immediately with saltines and lemon wedges. Garnish with chopped fresh parsley and scallions—and remember to provide a fork for each guest to remove clam meat from the shells.

RICK NAUG, APPLE CREEK SMOKERS

Since 1989, my company has been providing cooking woods to a variety of restaurants to prepare and flavor their various dishes. Early on, I realized that, to continue to stay on top of my market, I had to better understand how different woods enhanced or detracted from the flavors chefs were seeking. Our combined research turned up very little. (This was many years before Google.) I decided to do my own hands-on research, and any proper experiment requires a demanding venue. The competition barbecue circuit was, is, and always will be the most demanding venue of its kind. One competition led to another . . . and another . . . and another. I found I wasn't researching the wood anymore—I was hooked on how the "old masters" made barbecue the traditional way, low and slow.

Diva Q Planked Smoked Scallops with Tomatoes and Garlic

Serves 6

Diva Q's scallops as presented here on cedar in the raw will wow your guests' eyes, appetites, and palates. Thanks, and way to go, Danielle! You'll need six soaked cedar planks for this recipe, and they're a worthwhile investment. It's a nice presentation, and they add an interesting flavor you and your guests will enjoy.

2 pints cherry tomatoes, halved

12 cloves garlic

2 to 3 sprigs fresh thyme

1 cup olive oil

1 large sweet onion

6 fresh scallops (U10 or larger)

Sea salt and freshly ground black pepper

Finely chopped fresh chives

Preheat a charcoal grill to medium-high heat for indirect cooking.

Place the tomatoes, garlic, thyme, and olive oil in a disposable 9 by 12-inch aluminum pan (i.e., a half pan). Add 2 handfuls apple wood chips to the charcoal. Place the pan on the indirect side of the grill. Cover and cook until the tomatoes have taken on the smoke and have begun to break down.

Meanwhile, cut the onion in half and place it on the indirect side of the grill next to the pan of tomatoes. Cover and cook for about 30 minutes, opening the lid every 10 minutes and stirring the tomatoes. Remove the onion and pan from the grill and set aside.

Place a scallop in the center of each of 6 soaked cedar planks. Drizzle 1 tablespoon of the tomato olive oil and place 2 cloves of the garlic on top of each scallop. Sprinkle with sea salt and pepper. Cook over direct heat, covered, until the scallop just turns opaque, 15 to 20 minutes.

Serve the scallops with the remaining smoked tomatoes and garlic, the smoked onion, a sprinkling of chives, and a drizzle of tomato oil.

DANIELLE BENNETT DIMOVSKI, **DIVA Q**

Diva Q earned the title World Champion of Pork in 2011, and we're one of the highest-ranked Canadian barbecue teams in the Kansas City Barbeque Society. My passion for barbecue is second to none. I brake for barbecue whenever I spy a "BBQ" sign, be it at a roadside shack or a fancy rib joint. I'm raising three children with my husband in suburban Ontario, Canada, and I have a barbecue career that reaches far beyond the Canadian border. I compete and win awards in barbecue contests all over North America, including the Jack Daniel's World Championship Invitational Barbecue. As a Certified Barbeque Judge, I know the drill. Diva Q has been featured on TV and in print media of all varieties, and our website attracts more than a million visits annually.

The best backyard barbecues are the ones that are not planned down to the last minute and the ones that are spontaneous. On more than one summer day we have assembled a motley crew of friends and family and grilled anything in sight. Cold beverages, good tunes, and a laid-back attitude can go a long way toward having a blast. Set up assorted tables with multicolored tablecloths. Mason jars stand in for cups. It really doesn't matter what you serve. If it's honest, well-cooked food and you are with friends and family, then it's always going to be a terrific backyard party.

—Danielle Dimovski, Diva Q

Jim Erickson's Salmon Parmesan

Serves 2 to 4

When Jim Erickson of Beaver Castors (page 121) offers you a morsel from his barbecue pit, never turn him down. Your first bite will make you so glad you said, "Yes, please," to his "Would you like to try this?" His barbecue venison, bear, and elk are tender and moist. You'll taste smoke and Jim's secret seasonings, but you won't taste a strong gamy flavor, and you'll be hard put to guess what you're eating if he doesn't tell you before you take a bite. Follow Jim's directions here with planked salmon and you'll taste what we mean. Hints: This recipe will work with any species of salmon, but try to find line-caught wild salmon whenever possible. Try to avoid farm-raised Atlantic. Experiment with different types of wood planks. Western red cedar and alder are most commonly used in the Pacific Northwest, but Jim has also had great luck with cherry planks. While cooking, the planks should smolder, and a little flame emanating from the edges is not a problem.

⅓ cup mayonnaise

¼ cup plus 2 tablespoons freshly grated Parmesan cheese

1 shallot or ½ small yellow onion, finely chopped

1 clove garlic

2 tablespoons chopped fresh parsley

1 teaspoon dried oregano leaves, crushed

1 teaspoon dried rosemary, crushed

⅛ teaspoon salt

⅛ teaspoon freshly ground black pepper

1 (1-pound) salmon fillet, cut into serving-size pieces

Soak your cedar planks according to the manufacturer's directions and preheat a grill to 450°F.

Mix the mayonnaise, ¼ cup of the Parmesan cheese, the shallot, herbs, salt, and pepper in a small bowl.

Place the salmon on a soaked plank, leaving some space between the pieces. Spread the mayonnaise mixture evenly over the salmon. Sprinkle the remaining 2 tablespoons Parmesan cheese on top.

Place the plank on the grill over the hot coals or gas flame, close the lid, and cook for about 12 minutes, or until done. The white protein will have begun coming through to the surface of the salmon.

Note: You can also bake the salmon in a 450°F oven on an oiled baking sheet for the same amount of time.

JIM ERICKSON,
BEAVER CASTORS

I am the head cook of the Beaver Castors competition cooking team. My home is in the shadow of Mount Rainier in rural Pierce County, Washington. I am honored to have been credited for helping define Pacific Northwest cuisine. As a lifelong avid outdoorsman, I'm renowned for my fish and wildlife cooking, and camp cooking, in addition to competition barbecue. The first state championship I won was the Washington State Championship in 1988. After that, the Beaver Castors went on to succeed in the states of Oregon, Idaho, Montana, Tennessee, Kentucky, Florida, North Carolina, Texas, Oklahoma, Nevada, California, Missouri, Iowa, and Georgia, as well as the Canadian provinces of British Columbia and Alberta. The Beaver Castors were invited to the first American Royal Invitational and the first Jack Daniel's Invitational. Over the next 10 years the Beaver Castors became the only team in history to qualify for both of these prestigious events every year, and we were named Reserve Grand Champion at both contests in 1993. Our team has won a first place in every category these two contests require at one time or another. Every summer, I cook a beautiful whole hog and conduct a barbecue demonstration for the public at the Canadian National BBQ Championships in Whistler, British Columbia.

Rick Naug's Northwest Planked Salmon

Serves 4

According to Rick Naug (see page 117), the purpose of the plank is twofold: it's a barrier to the heat, and it offers an interesting flavor when subjected to the heat. The thicker the plank, the less chance of its charring before the fish is cooked to your taste. The plank can be of any wood—just make sure it is untreated. A ¾-inch thickness works best, but ½ inch or even ¼ inch would suffice. You can also use locally available fish instead of salmon.

1 (1-pound) salmon fillet, skin on, pinbones removed

1 tablespoon mayonnaise

½ teaspoon coarse kosher or sea salt

¼ teaspoon freshly cracked black pepper

1 lemon

About 30 minutes before cooking, rub a plank with olive oil and set aside. Keep adding olive oil as it is absorbed.

Place charcoal in a circular mound against the side of your grill, using at most half of the available inside area. Preheat to 450°F.

Place the fish skin side down on the plank. Brush it with mayonnaise, then season with the salt and pepper. Cut the lemon in half and reserve half for finishing the dish. Slice the other half and arrange the slices to cover the fillet.

Place the plank in the grill opposite the coals. Cover the grill and close all vents. Depending on the thickness of the fillet, cook for 15 to 20 minutes, testing until the fish flakes easily with a fork. Your fish should be opaque.

Remove from the cooker. Tent with foil and let rest for 5 minutes before serving. Squeeze the remaining lemon half over the fish and serve.

Seriously BBQ Sea Bass with Asparagus and Coriander, Lime, and Chili Pesto

Serves 4 to 6

This recipe is an inspiration for what you can do on your outdoor grill with a cast-iron skillet and locally available fish and other ingredients. Chef Jeremy (see page 30) makes a coriander/lime/chili pesto, but a basil/lemon pesto could serve equally well. Jeremy serves his with sautéed samphire, but since samphire is available fresh only in Europe, we've adapted the recipe to include fresh asparagus or Broccolini.

CORIANDER, LIME, AND CHILI PESTO

1 cup fresh cilantro leaves

½ cup extra virgin olive oil

2 tablespoons macadamia nuts

1 tablespoon freshly squeezed lime juice

¼ cup finely grated pecorino cheese

⅓ teaspoon sea salt or kosher salt

⅓ teaspoon hot red pepper flakes

Freshly ground black pepper

SEA BASS

2 to 4 pounds sea bass,
   lake bass, or bream

1 tablespoon sea salt or kosher salt

¼ cup extra virgin olive oil

5 tablespoons butter

1½ to 2 pounds asparagus or Broccolini

2 tablespoons freshly
   squeezed lemon juice

Make the pesto: Combine all the pesto ingredients, including black pepper to taste, in a blender and blend until smooth. Set aside.

Fillet the fish, leaving the skin on. Wash well, score the skin lightly, and rub sea salt into the incisions.

Heat the oil and 4 tablespoons of the butter in a large cast-iron grill pan over medium-high heat until rather hot. The oil allows the butter to reach a higher temperature without burning, and the butter enhances the flavor. Olive oil that cooks at high heat will be ruined. Place the fish skin side down in the pan and place a flat saucer on top of the fish to prevent the flesh from bowing and to allow the skin to crisp. The fish may look like it's getting too hot, and you may be afraid the skin side will burn, but that should not happen. The fish will start to become opaque in color, and this will give you around a minute before flipping and taking it off the heat. It will finish cooking by the time you lift it from the pan to the plate.

While the fish is cooking, drop the asparagus spears or Broccolini into boiling water and blanch them for 1 to 2 minutes. Remove, drain, and set aside.

Squeeze the lemon juice generously over the fish. Remove it from the pan and set aside.

Transfer the asparagus or Broccolini to the same pan the fish was in, add the remaining tablespoon of butter and some black pepper, and sauté until tender, 3 to 5 minutes.

Pour the pesto on the fish, top it with asparagus or Broccolini, and serve immediately.

Craig Whitson's ElvisLaks Grilled Salmon

Serves 6 to 8

As Craig Whitson told us, salmon is a popular dish in Norway, so he felt it was his patriotic responsibility to give you a salmon recipe worthy of the citizens of Norway and your backyard guests. Laks is the Norwegian word for salmon (kind of like the lox in bagels and lox). Craig had been cooking salmon for years, tweaking the recipe over time. When he made this recipe in Memphis in 2008, he received fourth place in the seafood category—hence the Elvis reference. Now his lucky students prepare this dish in Craig's cooking classes, and it is always a hit.

1 whole side salmon fillet
   (3½ to 4 pounds), skin on

Kosher salt and freshly
   ground black pepper

Sugar

1 cup coarse-grain mustard, such
   as Zatarain's Creole Mustard
   or something French

3 tablespoons dark beer or stout
   (aquavit is also good)

2 tablespoons finely chopped fresh
   dill, plus more for garnish

Light brown sugar

Sprinkle the salmon with kosher salt, pepper, and sugar. Let stand for 30 minutes.

Preheat a cooker to 250°F for indirect cooking.

Mix the mustard, beer, and 2 tablespoons of dill in a small bowl. Spread a thin, even layer of the mixture over the cut side of the salmon. Top the mustard mixture with light brown sugar. Don't be afraid to use too much, as the sugar will melt and form a glaze. Sprinkle more finely chopped fresh dill over the top.

Place the salmon on the grate over indirect heat, cover, and cook for 30 to 40 minutes, or until done. Check by lightly pressing the surface of the thickest part of the salmon. This fish should be firm to the touch—not mushy and definitely not hard. If you are unsure, just cut a slit in the fish to check doneness. We won't tell anyone you did it.

Notes: Use wood chips (apple, cherry) or cedar planks to give a smokier flavor to the salmon.

You can also cook the salmon in portion sizes. Remember that smaller pieces will need less time on the grill.

CRAIG WHITSON, NORWAY

In 2004, Bjørn Tore Teigen, Espen Lynghaug, and I (and a few others) attended the American Royal in Kansas City. We wanted to observe how a barbecue competition worked because we were establishing the Norwegian championship for grilling.

We attended a judging class, tasted dozens of sauces, met a lot of interesting people, and ate a lot of barbecue. It didn't take many hours before Bjørn Tore and I understood that we definitely had to attend another competition and that next time around we'd be competing. Being an observer was fun and we learned a good deal, but we'd been bitten by the bug.

Three years later we attended our first Memphis in May competition and won third place in Exotic (using lamb, which is the premier meat in Norway). We've been back every year since, and today we feel very much a part of the world of competition barbecue.

CHAPTER 5: Barbecue champions take their sides as seriously as their main dishes. In fact, the sides they are sharing with you in this chapter are good enough to stand alone as a main course. Vegetarians could build a satisfying feast from many of the nonmeat dishes—or leave out the meat and still have a delicious meal: Bob's Never-Fail Romaine Salad, minus meat, for example. Or Scottie Johnson's Roasted Pesto Corn Salad. We received two recipes for baked potatoes that were similar but both so good we couldn't say no—to seconds or to the recipes. Maybe one or the other will become part of your permanent recipe collection.

Although sides aren't factored in for Grand Champion points in most contests, don't think for a minute that they are not important to the champs. Cash prize or not, a blue ribbon and trophy in sides is a cherished award with bragging rights. Have our champs given you some prize winning sides in this chapter? We say yes, but you and your backyard barbecue guests will be the judge.

Sides

Bob Lyon's Never-Fail Romaine Salad

Serves 6 to 8

Along with a meat and sauce recipe from Stein and Davis's book *All About BAR-B-Q Kansas City-Style*, this salad was the unanimous choice of five people who put together four to six issues of a barbecue newsletter for 10 years. Romaine lettuce is tossed with fresh garlic, scallions, thinly sliced pepperoni, pepper, cheddar, and balsamic vinegar—what a feast! Take out the meat and you still have a feast— but only if you're a vegetarian. The grilled and sauced steak with pepperoni enhancements are an omnivore's delight!

¼ to ½ cup extra virgin olive oil

4 or more cloves garlic, pressed

2 heads romaine lettuce

2 to 3 scallions, thinly sliced

Freshly ground black pepper

8 ounces pepperoni rounds, thinly sliced

4 to 6 ounces grated aged cheddar cheese

Balsamic vinegar, for serving

Pour the olive oil into a large salad bowl 2 hours before serving so the bottom of the bowl is covered. Press the garlic cloves into the oil and spread the pieces around. Guests should be able to smell the garlic as they arrive.

Separate the romaine leaves, rinse, and tear into large bite-sized pieces. Place the romaine in the bowl and swish around by hand until all the pieces are coated with the oil. Next, sprinkle the scallion pieces on top of the romaine and add a few twists of freshly ground black pepper. Then add the sliced pepperoni, followed by the grated cheese. Finally, drizzle balsamic vinegar on top. Do not toss the salad; all the good stuff will fall to the bottom.

Scottie Johnson's Roasted Pesto Corn Salad

Serves 4

Vegetarians, listen up! You could make a complete, delicious meal with this salad. The flavor of fresh corn made sweet from grilling, combined with a scallion/cilantro/pistachio pesto makes an over-the-top delicious salad. For balanced protein, add a small can of drained black beans if you must. Scottie serves it with Shrimp-Stuffed Avocados (page 116).

4 ears fresh corn, shucked

3 tablespoons extra virgin olive oil

Kosher salt and freshly
    ground black pepper

¼ cup sliced scallions, white
    and green parts

2 tablespoons shelled pistachios

¼ cup chopped fresh cilantro

Preheat a grill to medium-high.

Rub the corn with 1 tablespoon of the olive oil and season with salt and freshly ground black pepper. Place the corn on the grill and cook, uncovered, over direct heat until the kernels start to brown and soften, 10 to 12 minutes. Remove from the grill and set aside.

Place the scallions, pistachios, cilantro, and the remaining olive oil in a food processor and process until minced. Transfer to a medium serving bowl. Slice the corn kernels from the cobs and place them in the bowl. Toss the corn and cilantro pesto to mix well. Serve immediately.

SCOTTIE JOHNSON, CANCERSUCKSCHICAGO.COM

My wife, Corliss, was diagnosed with cancer in 2001. She went for chemo every Thursday for 1½ years, and she wore a "Cancer Sucks!" button to each treatment. She never let cancer get in her way, and she never put herself first. She wanted our family to be as normal as could be. Cancer finally beat her on February 2, 2003.

Because of the age of my girls at the time, 5 and not quite 2 years old, I knew I had to make a difference and try to preserve that bond with their mommy. She wouldn't be there physically, but she would be there spiritually. I also didn't want any other family to have to go through what we did as a family, so one year after dealing with our loss, I set up the Corliss Johnson Memorial Foundation to raise money for cancer research and to assist those fighting cancer. Her memory could live on through the foundation for my girls.

I had taken up backyard barbecuing and was starting to take it a little more seriously. Corliss was always my biggest fan, and we had plans for competing and eventually doing something with barbecue as an income. In 2005, I cooked two contests under the team name Corliss Johnson Memorial Foundation. In 2006, I changed the team name to cancersuckschicago.com. We donate profits to the foundation. The money that we can win at a contest isn't going to make me rich or allow me to retire, but it can help others.

Jaan's "Something from Nothing" Salad

Serves 8 to 10

Jaan (see page 96) told us that in the early 1990s food was scarce in Estonian supermarkets. He developed this recipe during his student days, when frugality was a necessity. He rediscovered it later, when his culinary career was beginning to blossom. We don't know if Jaan's success with this salad flows from luck or his outstanding culinary skills. Probably both, since more often than not "something from nothing" can yield a culinary dud. Feel free to do a little experimenting yourself, using what you have on hand, and maybe you'll discover your own something from nothing.

2 pounds green cabbage

1 cup mayonnaise

2 teaspoons spicy Russian mustard

1 teaspoon salt

1 teaspoon sugar

8 ounces sharp white cheddar cheese, or any cheese you have on hand, grated

Cut the cabbage into workable-size chunks and grate or chop them into fine pieces. Place the cabbage in a large bowl.

In a small bowl, mix the mayonnaise, mustard, salt, and sugar. Add the dressing to the cabbage and toss to coat. Cover and refrigerate for at least 4 hours to let the seasonings work. Gently mix in the cheese just before serving.

BBQ Freaks Chayote and Mango Slaw

Serves 6 to 8

When you're tired of the same old coleslaw, here's a new one that will wow your guests.

The tropical flavors deliver a complementary contrast to any barbecue, including grilled hot dogs, but especially burgers, pulled pork, ribs, or steak. You can still keep your old standby slaw, especially for family gatherings to continue your traditions, but don't pass this one up! If chayote is hard to find in your area, substitute jícama. They are both available in Latin markets.

DRESSING

1 tablespoon honey

1 teaspoon hot red pepper flakes

¼ cup extra virgin olive oil

Juice of 2 limes

¼ cup apple cider vinegar

SALAD

1 chayote, julienned

½ medium red onion, julienned

1 mango, peeled, pitted, and julienned

1 tomato, seeded and diced

1 tablespoon chopped fresh cilantro

Make the dressing: Whisk together all the ingredients in a small bowl and set aside.

Make the salad: Toss the ingredients together in a large bowl. Just before serving, pour on the dressing and toss to coat.

JOSE BENGOA, YOLANDA BOLIVAR, AND GABRIEL ANTUNEZ, BBQ FREAKS

Since 2006, we have been competing in championship barbecue competitions. Jose and Gabriel graduated from the French Culinary Institute, Yolanda from Johnson & Wales University. We came together because of our passion for food, music, and beer.

We started by accident, volunteering at the Jack Daniel's Puerto Rico barbecue contest, representing the specialty food store where we work. The adrenaline rush and the challenge it provided gave us the best time of our lives. We came in second overall and were hooked. Since Puerto Rico has beautiful 80-degree weather year-round, we get a lot of practice. Our families may be tired of our obsession, but we keep perfecting our recipes anyway. They don't seem to mind when they get to eat all the leftovers.

TOM AND MICHELE PERELKA, LO'-N-SLO' BBQ

Watching the Food Network and jokingly saying "I can do that" turned into a competitive hobby. For my (Tom) fortieth birthday, my wife, Michele, bought me an inexpensive offset smoker. After several modifications, we were able to dial the cooker in and produce some good barbecue. Before deciding to compete, we attended a local competition and got to experience what competition barbecue was really all about (friendliness and helpfulness). Our first official contest and win was in 2006, when our team earned a fourth-place rib call. Lo'-N-Slo' BBQ was hooked. From that first inexpensive smoker, to multiple smokers and trailers today, we haven't looked back.

Since 2006 Lo'-N-Slo' BBQ has earned 11 Grand Championships, 8 Reserve Grand Championships, 3 Grilling Grand Championships, and more than 200 top-ten category calls. Earning an invitation to the 2009 21st Annual Jack Daniel's World Championship Invitational earned us a second-place finish in the Cook's Choice category; then our 2010 invitation earned us a first-place Cook's Choice with a Perfect 180 Score. In 2011, we took home the PA State Cup. Our wins prove that not only are we champions of the four main Kansas City Barbeque Society categories but our team is also diverse in all food categories. Living by Gordon Ramsay's statement—"Be the best or go home; nobody ever talks about the second best dish they've ever tasted"—motivates us to excel in every contest. Ask our competitors—they will tell you!

Lo'-N-Slo' Grilled Asparagus

Serves 4 to 6

Although Lo'-N-Slo' gave us this recipe to go with their meat loaf (page 94) and garlic mashed potatoes (page 140), it is so delicious and goes so well with many other main courses that we put it in the sides chapter. Here's proof again that simple and easy is not to be ignored.

1 pound asparagus

½ cup olive oil

Salt and freshly ground black pepper

Rinse the asparagus spears and trim off the root ends. Place in a zipper bag. Add the olive oil and season with salt and pepper. Seal the bag tightly, then shake to completely coat the asparagus. Let rest for 10 minutes.

Prepare a grill to cook over direct heat.

Remove the asparagus from the bag and place it directly on the grill grates or on a grill pan over the hot coals. Cook for 2 minutes, then turn and cook for 2 minutes more, or until done but still a little crunchy. Do not overcook. Asparagus gets mushy and loses its bright green color when overcooked.

Gaelic Gourmet CAM Onion Bread Pudding

Serves 6

Carolyn Wells, Amy Winn, and Marty Lynch (see page 83) collaborated on this recipe years ago, adapting it from a Rick Browne recipe for onion pudding. Add a little of this and a little of that, taste it, and try again, until finally it's perfect! What to call it? Why not C for Carolyn, A for Amy, and M for Marty. Another star recipe was born. We've enjoyed this at contests and backyard barbecues ever since the CAM crew gave us the recipe. It is so rich with bread, cheese, eggs, and a pitmasterful balance of seasonings that we could make a meal of it—and have been known to do so.

8 tablespoons (1 stick) butter

1 tablespoon olive oil

8 cups thinly sliced Vidalia or
    Texas sweet onions

¼ cup dry vermouth (optional)

1 clove garlic, crushed

6 cups French bread in 1-inch chunks

6 cups grated Emmenthaler
    or Swiss cheese

3 eggs

1½ cups half-and-half

1 teaspoon sea salt or kosher salt

Freshly ground black pepper

Preheat a gas grill to 400° to 500°F or a charcoal grill until hot. Melt half of the butter with the olive oil in a cast-iron skillet on the grill. Add the onions, cover the skillet, and move it to a cooler zone to simmer for 15 minutes.

Uncover the skillet, move it to a medium-heat zone, and stir occasionally until the onions caramelize, about 20 minutes. Add the vermouth, if using, and garlic and continue heating until the liquid evaporates, stirring constantly for 10 to 15 minutes. Remove the onion mixture from the skillet and transfer it to a large bowl.

Clean the skillet, then spray the sides and bottom with nonstick cooking spray. Add the bread and toast, stirring well to brown all sides. Spread the onion mixture in the pan. Melt the remaining butter and pour it over the bread and onion mixture. Sprinkle the cheese on top.

In a medium bowl, lightly beat the eggs and add the half-and-half and salt and pepper. Pour this over the bread, onion, and cheese mixture. Use a spatula to lift the bread to make sure the liquid is infused throughout. Place the skillet on the grill. Using the indirect heat method, cook for 30 to 40 minutes, until puffed and golden brown. When the pudding is done, remove it from the grill, cut it into large triangles, and serve.

Craig Whitson's Cipolle Agrodolce

Makes 2 pounds

Craig Whitson (see page 125), of Norway, sent us this Italian recipe for pickled onions. They are great served with grilled fish or meat. You could try them with Craig's ElvisLaks (page 124) or as an appetizer served with sourdough bread. Craig admits that he always steals a few extra from the bowl while nobody is looking.

2 pounds pearl onions or other
    small onions, peeled

1½ cups dry red wine

½ cup water

1 cup red wine vinegar

2 bay leaves

Grated zest of 1 lemon

¼ cup sugar

½ teaspoon salt

Place all the ingredients in a large pot and bring to a boil over medium-high heat. Reduce the heat and simmer until the sauce becomes thick and syrupy, 1 to 1½ hours. Watch carefully as the sauce thickens. A couple of minutes too long and it will burn.

Let cool in the pot. If desired, cover and refrigerate for 1 hour before serving.

Burnin' Bob's Butts N Bones Smoked Beans

Serves 25

Although their team name is Burnin' Bob's Butts N Bones, Bob and Donna Oldfield could also earn the title Butts N Beans for this outstanding Rocky Mountains bean recipe. The mix of beans, condiments, onion, bell pepper, meat, and spices, smoked for hours in a barbecue pit, makes one of the best side dishes you'll ever taste east, west, north, or south of Pikes Peak!

7 pounds, more or less, navy beans cooked from scratch or canned pork and beans, drained and rinsed

1 cup packed brown sugar

½ cup ketchup

½ cup hot barbecue sauce

1½ cups mild barbecue sauce

⅓ cup prepared mustard

1 medium red onion, diced and sautéed until soft

½ cup diced green bell pepper

2 teaspoons ground cumin

½ teaspoon salt

½ teaspoon freshly ground black pepper

2 teaspoons Tabasco or your favorite hot sauce

1 pound chopped smoked pork butt or brisket (such as Paul Schatte's brisket, page 82, or Flyboy brisket, page 80)

Preheat your smoker to 250°F.

Combine all the ingredients in a heavy cast-iron or enamel 6-quart Dutch oven. Smoke, uncovered, for 3 hours, stirring every hour.

BOB AND DONNA OLDFIELD, BURNIN' BOB'S BUTTS N BONES

Our first barbecue competition as the Butts N Bones team was in 2003 at the Frisco Colorado BBQ Challenge. We were inspired to form our team after sampling barbecue from some teams at a barbecue contest in Denver. Donna said, "I can do better than this." So we bought a small offset smoker and proceeded to ruin about three hundred pounds of meat before we decided we were ready to compete.

We packed everything on a flatbed trailer and headed up the hill. It didn't take long to realize we weren't quite ready for competition cooking, but we made turn-ins and waited for results. We ended up 48th out of 54 teams but weren't ready to give up.

Since that day, we have won a number of Grand Championships around the country and found a whole new family of great barbecue people. We are also doing competition cooking classes, with hopes of getting more people involved in barbecue—hopefully with fewer failures than we saw in our early days.

Paul Schatte's Head Country II Pinto Beans Cilantro Style

Serves 20

We could eat beans every day, especially when Paul Schatte is the cook. Now, thanks to Paul, you can enjoy one of his masterpieces at your next backyard barbecue. Here he marries traditional barbecue beans ingredients with a surprise flavor: fresh cilantro. We love it!

4 (15-ounce) cans pinto beans

8 ounces chopped barbecued meat or sliced sausage (optional)

1 (16-ounce) can diced tomatoes

1 medium white onion, chopped

1 green bell pepper, cored, seeded, and chopped

⅓ cup pickled jaleños

3 tablespoons Head Country All Purpose Championship Seasoning or your favorite seasoning

1 tablespoon ground cumin

1 tablespoon chili powder

½ cup chopped fresh cilantro

Preheat the oven to 350°F.

Drain most of the juice from the can of beans and pour the beans into a deep 9 by 12-inch aluminum pan (i.e., a half pan). Add the meat tomatoes, onion, green pepper, jalapeños, seasoning, cumin, and chili powder. Stir well to blend. Cover the pan with foil. Bake for 2 hours, until hot and bubbling. Right before serving, remove the foil and stir in the cilantro.

I have had the privilege of cooking barbecue for Garth Brooks, Roy Clark, the PGA tour when it came through Oklahoma, the governors' convention when it was held in Oklahoma, and many others. When people come up to me and say that was the best barbecue they ever tasted, that makes me proud.

—Paul Schatte, Head Country II

Jamie K's Hominy Casserole

Serves 6 to 8

Koz told us they can't make enough of this. "It is so simple, but unbelievably delicious. People always rave about it and ask for more," he told us. He credits Jamie with the recipe. If you think you don't like hominy, you'd better try this casserole. We think you'll be saying, "Except for Jamie's casserole, I don't care much for hominy."

2 tablespoons butter

1 medium yellow onion, chopped

Dash of salt

Dash of freshly ground black pepper

Dash of garlic salt

1 (10.75-ounce) can cream of mushroom soup

1 (8-ounce) jar Cheez Whiz

1 (4-ounce) can green chiles

3 (15-ounce) cans hominy, drained

1 bag potato chips, crushed

Preheat a grill to 350°F for indirect cooking.

Melt the butter in a large skillet over medium heat. Add the onion and sauté until translucent, 3 to 5 minutes. Season with salt, pepper, and garlic salt. Stir in the cream of mushroom soup, Cheez Whiz, and chiles and cook until the mixture reaches a bare simmer. Place the hominy in a large aluminum pan or 6-quart cast-iron Dutch oven and pour the mixture over the hominy.

Cover the pan, place on the grill, close the lid, and cook for 30 to 45 minutes, or until hot and bubbling. Sprinkle the crushed potato chips over the top and cook, uncovered, for about 10 minutes more, or until the chips are toasted.

DARIAN AND JAMIE KHOSRAVI, KOSMO'S Q

One thing I am to a tee is a true competitor. When I found out that a BBQ competition was going to be held near our hometown, I could not resist the urge. I signed up and loaded the minivan and headed in. Competition BBQ was a mere bucket list item at the time, but after a tenth-place rib call and 48 hours of no sleep I was hooked!

4 Legs Up BBQ Not Yo' Mama's Mac and Cheese

Serves 8 to 10

Since mac and cheese is a classic American dish loved by all, there are many contenders for the best recipe. We have enjoyed many wannabes, and as an obligation to our readers we'll try any new ones within reach. We'll always rank this one up there with the best, however. Mama never put chiles in her mac and cheese. We're glad Kelly and Roni (see page 45) did!

4 tablespoons (½ stick) butter

¼ cup all-purpose flour

1 medium yellow onion, minced

1 (28-ounce) can chopped green chiles

4 cups whole milk

1 pound Velveeta, cut into small cubes

2 cups shredded Colby or
  Monterey Jack cheese

1 pound small pasta shells

Melt the butter in a 2-quart stockpot or Dutch oven over medium heat. Add the flour and cook for 2 minutes, stirring constantly. Add the onion and cook until tender, stirring frequently. Add the green chiles and cook until heated through. Add the milk and bring just to a boil.

Reduce the heat to a simmer, add the cubed Velveeta, and stir until melted. Add the shredded cheese 1 cup at a time until melted. Keep warm.

Heat a smoker or grill to 350°F.

Cook the pasta shells according to the package directions until just before they are al dente. Drain the pasta, add it to the cheese sauce, and mix well.

Pour the mac and cheese into a greased foil half pan (9 by 12 inches). Place it in the smoker or on the grill and cook for about 1 hour, or until bubbling.

Cruzen 2 Que Grilled Stuffed Potatoes

Serves 6

John and Peggy routinely serve these potatoes to contest guests and backyard barbecue guests. Friends count on it, and you can't let friends down. Here's another dish so rich in flavor and protein that we could eat several and call it a meal! They're even better topped with bacon bits, diced jalapeños, sour cream, or your own favorite add-ons.

3 baking potatoes

Olive oil

DennyMikes Fintastic Savory Seafood Seasoning or Old Bay Seasoning

3 tablespoons butter

3 tablespoons sour cream

¼ to ⅓ cup milk

2 tablespoons freshly grated Parmesan cheese

1 to 2 tablespoons chopped fresh chives (optional)

1 teaspoon garlic powder

Salt and freshly ground black pepper

Grated cheddar cheese, for serving

Paprika

Prepare a medium-hot to hot grill.

Scrub the potatoes, rub them with olive oil, and then season with DennyMikes Fintastic or Old Bay seasoning. Wrap the potatoes in foil and grill, covered, for 1 hour, turning after 30 minutes so the skins don't burn. Leave the grill on.

Remove the potatoes from the foil, cut them in half, scoop out the flesh, and place in a large mixing bowl. Set the potato skins aside. Mash the potatoes with the butter. With a mixer on medium speed, beat the potatoes. Add the sour cream and then enough milk to form a mashed potato consistency. Add the Parmesan cheese, chives, if using, garlic powder, and salt and pepper to taste.

Stuff the potatoes back into the skins. Top with cheddar cheese, then sprinkle with paprika. Place them back on the grill (either directly on the grate or in an aluminum pan) and cook until heated through and the cheese melts, 15 to 20 minutes.

JOHN AND PEGGY VANDERCRUYSSEN, CRUZEN 2 QUE

I have been grilling and smoking food for many years. About 8 years ago I attended a barbecue competition with a friend in New Holland, Pennsylvania, and was hooked! After competing for 3 years, sleeping in my truck, and towing my grill, we bought an RV, and now the entire family goes, along with our Newfoundland dog and two Bengal cats! We have traveled as far north as Maine for a competition and as far south as Georgia—having a blast!

Lo'-N-Slo' Roasted Garlic Twice-Baked Potatoes

Serves 6

For all of you who like garlic, this is what we call down-home cookin'! Roasted garlic, butter, sour cream, and Parmesan cheese make these potatoes exceptionally delicious. Lo'-N-Slo' (see page 132) serves these on the side with the team's meat loaf (page 94) and Grilled Asparagus (page 132), but you'll find that it pairs well with almost any backyard barbecue fare. Now and then we add some pulled pork or burnt ends to make it a meal in itself.

1 head garlic

Olive oil, for drizzling

Salt and freshly ground black pepper

6 medium baking potatoes

8 tablespoons (1 stick) butter

1 cup sour cream

2 to 3 tablespoons milk, or as needed

Salt and freshly ground black pepper

Shredded Parmesan cheese, for topping

Prepare a hot grill for indirect cooking or preheat the oven to 350°F.

Make the roasted garlic: Cut ¼ to ½ inch off the top of the head of garlic. Place the garlic on a piece of foil large enough to wrap around the entire head. Drizzle the olive oil over the cut end and season with salt and pepper. Wrap tightly in foil. Place on the grill, opposite the coals, close the lid, and roast for 30 to 40 minutes. If using the oven, bake for 30 minutes.

Prepare the potatoes: Scrub the potatoes under cold water and pat them dry. Use a fork to poke holes in the potatoes, then place them, unwrapped, on the grill opposite the coals. Cook for 45 to 60 minutes, turning every 10 minutes. The potatoes can also be baked in a 350°F oven for the same amount of time. If you're pressed for time, you can put the potatoes in the microwave for 2 to 3 minutes and then wrap and grill them for 20 to 30 minutes. Leave the grill on.

Remove the potatoes from the grill and let cool for 10 minutes so they are easier to handle. Meanwhile, heat the butter, sour cream, and milk in a saucepan over low heat, just to take the chill off. Halve the potatoes lengthwise, then scoop out the centers, leaving ⅛ inch on the skin. Place the scooped-out potatoes in a medium bowl. Separate the garlic cloves and squeeze the roasted garlic from the skins into the bowl. Lightly mix the potatoes and garlic, then place the mixture in a ricer and rice into another bowl. Pour the heated milk mixture over the riced potatoes and mix. Season with salt and pepper.

Scoop the potato mixture into the reserved potato skins and top with Parmesan cheese. Put the filled skins back on the grill opposite the coals. Cover and cook for 5 minutes.

KCass American Royal Potato Salad

Serves 6 to 8

There's potato salad, and then there's POTATO SALAD!!! This one from Rich and Bunny Tuttle, of KCass BBQ Team (see page 85), pays tribute to the American Royal Barbecue, the World Series of Barbecue. We guarantee that this one is good enough to measure up to the title.

8 Yukon Gold potatoes, cut
into ½-inch cubes

1 (10-ounce) Kraft Philadelphia
Savory Garlic Cooking Creme

1 (10.75-ounce) can cream of celery soup

1½ pounds Velveeta, cut into small cubes

1 (5-ounce) container Athenos
blue cheese crumbles

½ cup shredded pepper Jack cheese

½ cup shredded Colby cheese

¼ cup shredded Parmesan cheese

2 tablespoons Golden Toad Prime
Steak Rub or your favorite rub

1 teaspoon Crystal Hot Sauce (not Tabasco)

1 teaspoon of your favorite steak sauce

¼ to ½ cup milk

Panko breadcrumbs, for topping

Boil the potatoes until al dente, then throw in cold water to stop the cooking process. Drain and set aside.

Preheat the oven to 350°F.

Combine the cooking creme, soup, Velveeta, all the cheeses, the rub, hot sauce, and steak sauce in the top of a double boiler over medium heat. Cook until the cheeses are melted, stirring often, 15 to 20 minutes. Add enough milk to thin the mixture (it usually needs all of it).

Place the potatoes in a greased 9 by 13-inch baking dish. Pour the cheesy mixture over the cooled potatoes, sprinkle with panko, and bake for 20 to 30 minutes, or until hot and bubbling.

Preheat the broiler and place the dish under it for a few minutes to brown the panko. Serve hot.

CHAPTER 6: Remember back in your high-school days when someone substituted salt for sugar and sugar for salt in your favorite teen diner or hamburger joint? If you've ever fallen victim to this practical joke, you're probably not laughing. It illustrates the point, however, that seasonings make a difference. What you put them on and how much you put on it will either complement or ruin the food you are eating.

There are two camps when the question of barbecue sauce and other seasonings comes up. Most competition barbecuers will swear that "the secret is in the sauce." Or the rub, mop, sop, marinade, or brine. A few, definitely in the minority, will say, "My barbecue is so good it doesn't need any sauce!" We have yet to hear that remark from a champ on the competition network.

Great philosophical culinary issues such as this have no right or wrong answers. It's a matter of personal taste and opinion. Fortunately, this is an issue that you can decide for yourself with your own palate. If you're like us, you'll taste some seasoned barbecue that is out-of-this-world fantastic. Likewise you'll taste some unseasoned barbecue that is fabulous!

Rubs, Marinades, Mops, Sops, and Sauces

IN THIS CHAPTER THE SPOTLIGHT IS ON SEASONINGS YOU CAN EXPERIMENT WITH IN PUMPING UP YOUR BACKYARD BARBECUE DISHES. AS WITH ALL RECIPES, WE ENCOURAGE YOU TO START WITH THE BASIC RECIPE AS IS, THEN TWEAK WITH OTHER INGREDIENTS OR OMISSIONS, AND ADJUST QUANTITIES, TO SUIT YOUR OWN TASTE. THE POSSIBILITIES ARE ENDLESS.

BBQ SEASONINGS PRIMER

Rub: A rub is a dry spice or a combination of dry spices, from just salt and pepper to any concoction you can dream up to season whatever you are going to smoke or grill. Like marinades, rubs add flavor to your meat before you cook it. Normally you season with dry rubs before cooking, not during or after.

Moisture, light, and heat aren't good for rubs, so store them in a cool, dry, dark place. They'll keep for 2 to 3 months that way or for up to 6 months in the freezer. We like to put our rub in a clean plastic shaker bottle to make it easy to store and use.

Marinade: A marinade is a liquid mixture usually composed of an acidic ingredient, such as vinegar, wine, or fruit juice, and a more neutral one, such as water or oil, along with various spices and herbs. You soak your meat in it for anywhere from 1 to 24 hours before cooking, and it's particularly important and useful in grilling because the high, intense heats can dry out your meat.

The acid in marinades helps protect meat from the formation of harmful bacteria, but it is no excuse to ignore the rules of safe food handling. Always marinate meat in the refrigerator to prevent bacteria from forming and do not baste meat with used marinade that has not been boiled for at least 2 to 3 minutes to kill any harmful bacteria.

salt &

Brine: At its most basic, brine is a solution of water and salt, though some brines include sugar and other spices. You may need to heat the brine to dissolve the seasonings, but cool it to room temperature before using it so that the hot brine doesn't begin to cook the meat. Meat is soaked in brine in the refrigerator for varying lengths of time, based on the size of the cut.

Brined meat is more moist and flavorful than meat that has not been brined. After you remove ribs from brine, rinse them to remove excess salt, then pat dry. You may also want to reduce the amount of salt in your rub.

Sops, Mops, and Bastes: Sops, mops, and bastes all are basically the same thing. Back in the old days, before we were barbecuing, the meat had a tendency to dry out. So our forebears concocted a flavorful liquid to apply to the dry meat. They dipped clean rags in the liquid and sopped it on the meat. Then came the dish mop to apply the liquid, so it was a mop. Now we just call it a baste, and most of us apply it using a garden mister so we can adjust the spray.

You may want to use either straight apple juice or a mixture of half apple cider vinegar and half apple juice to help retain moisture during cooking. We prefer apple juice, which won't change the flavor of the meat. Try both ways and make your own decision. Either of these bases also works well to put down flare-ups.

Sauces and Glazes: A sauce is a seasoned liquid barbecue condiment. Popular bases are tomato, vinegar, and mustard; soy sauce, mayonnaise, pureed fruit, and other liquid ingredients are also used.

A glaze is basically a sauce brushed on the meat as it finishes cooking. You can make it yourself, or it can be as simple as a store-bought barbecue sauce that you brush on a slab of ribs during the last 30 minutes of cooking.

Some combine their barbecue sauces with a light honey, such as clover, or another sweetener such as brown sugar or agave, usually in a 2:1 ratio (2 barbecue sauce to 1 sweetener).

Mope & Dope Beef Rub

Makes about 2 cups

Although Kevin and Scott built this rub specifically for beef, we recommend that you try it on other meats as an all-purpose rub. We've enjoyed it on fried potatoes, scrambled eggs, and other nonbarbecue foods. Go for it!

¾ cup sugar

½ cup fine canning or pickling salt

¼ cup garlic powder

¼ cup paprika

2 tablespoons ground black pepper

2 tablespoons chili powder

1 tablespoon onion powder

1 teaspoon dry mustard

1 teaspoon ground ginger

1 teaspoon ground cumin

1 teaspoon cayenne

Combine all the ingredients in an airtight container and mix well. The rub will keep, covered and stored away from heat, light, and moisture, for up to 6 months.

KEVIN HULS AND SCOTT LARSON, MOPE & DOPE SMOKERS

We both love to cook. One day Kevin had an idea about building a smoker. So he went on YouTube and learned how to build one from scratch. I took the easy way and bought one that was already built. One day Kevin did some samples of meat for people in a local watering hole in town. The people loved the samples of ribs, pork shoulder, and beef roast. Then we started to make our wieners and brats too. One day, in 2011, Kevin had an idea to enter a barbecue competition at a local fair, so we did, and took second place, just one point out of first. There were eight teams in the competition (it was the first year).

We've done other things, such as a music festival and church festival. At the music festival we just did hamburgers, hot dogs, and brats. At the church festival we did barbecue ribs that everyone liked. After that, we both got a bright idea about starting a website that tells about what we do and where people can leave comments about the food that they had. The website is www.mopeand dopesmokers.com.

Dick's Tricks Dirty Dick's Barbecue Spice

Makes about 2 cups

When a champ like Dirty Dick turns loose of a rub recipe, everyone pays attention. We're not saying Richard is giving away one of his top secrets here, but we're not saying he isn't. The balance of kosher salt with brown sugar carries the other seasonings straight to your palate, with crowd-pleasing and barbecue-judge-pleasing results.

6 tablespoons kosher salt

6 tablespoons light brown sugar

¼ cup paprika

3 tablespoons chili powder

2 tablespoons freshly ground black pepper

1½ tablespoons garlic powder

1 tablespoon lemon pepper

1 tablespoon dried thyme, crushed

1 tablespoon dried tarragon, crushed

1 teaspoon onion powder

1 teaspoon ground cumin

Mix all the ingredients together thoroughly and sift through a strainer twice. Transfer to an airtight container. The barbecue spice will keep, stored away from heat, light, and moisture, for up to 6 months.

RICHARD WESTHAVER, DIRTY DICK AND THE LEGLESS WONDERS

My son Rick (the first Junior World BBQ Champion), Jean Brown, and a revolving menagerie of family and friends compete together as part of Dirty Dick and the Legless Wonders. By day I am a horticulturist with my own interior landscaping company, Mister Green Jeans. By night I'm a barbecue chef extraordinaire, who has won more than 300 awards since 1991, including the Jack Daniel's World Championship Invitational Barbecue. I also manufacture my own award-winning hot sauce called, curiously enough, Dirty Dick's Hot Pepper Sauce (www.dirtydickshotsauce.com).

In 1982, after attending a barbecue festival in Memphis, I took my barbecue hobby up a notch. I started building grills (I now have twelve in my backyard). I built two stainless-steel smokers, started trying different types of wood to infuse their flavors into various meats, and built a 120-gallon stainless-steel tank that I now take with me on the road as my grill pit at various barbecue competitions.

Our memorable team name is derived from my nickname, "Dirty Dick," and my firefighter friends, who partied so heavily that by midnight on Friday they'd be swaying back and forth, ready to fall down, so I'd call them the "legless wonders."

Dirty Dick's General-Purpose Marinade

Makes about 1¼ cups

Richard (see page 147) assured us that this is "a good one!" We agree. The mix of sweet, sour, and spicy will complement any meat you are grilling or smoking. According to Richard, "It will make a mop handle taste good!" We don't recommend wasting it on a mop handle.

½ cup packed brown sugar

½ cup olive oil

¼ cup balsamic vinegar

4 cloves garlic, crushed

3 tablespoons grainy mustard

2 tablespoons Dirty Dick's Hot Pepper Sauce or your favorite hot sauce

2 tablespoons grated lemon zest

2 tablespoons grated orange zest

1 tablespoon kosher salt

Combine all of the ingredients in a medium mixing bowl and blend well with a wire whisk.

Immerse meat in the marinade overnight in the refrigerator. The next day, bring the meat to room temperature, pat dry, then season and grill or smoke as desired.

BBQ Freaks Seasoned Salt

Makes about 1¾ cups

Thyme, garlic, and smoked paprika give this salt from BBQ Freaks (see page 131) a signature flavor that will complement most of your backyard barbecue meats or sides. Save it for one or the other, however, so that the one dish you use it in will have that BBQ Freaks mystique.

¼ cup coarsely ground black pepper

¼ cup granulated garlic

1 cup kosher salt

2 tablespoons dried thyme, crushed

2 tablespoons dried pimentón de la vera, aka Spanish smoked paprika (available online and at gourmet specialty stores)

Combine all the ingredients in an airtight container and mix well. The seasoned salt will keep, covered and stored away from heat, light, and moisture, for up to 6 months.

Jaan's Estonian Black Currant Barbecue Mop Sauce

Makes 3 to 4 cups

This sauce has won awards as a mop sauce for beef loin and spareribs and, as a stand-alone sauce, served hot as an accompaniment to meat. According to Jaan, "It was first brewed a dozen years ago and named after Luigendi, a farm in Estonia, where our barbecue association was founded. Luigendi was the home of the first president of the association at that time, Tiit Treve." When Jaan modified the recipe as it appears here, he called it, "First Lady's Modified," because the president's wife was the first to mix it.

1 pound (4 sticks) unsalted butter

1 cup dark beer

1 pound black currants (fresh or frozen)

4 ounces rhubarb (fresh or frozen)

1 teaspoon salt

1 teaspoon juniper berries, crushed

1 teaspoon dried thyme, crushed

1 teaspoon dried rosemary, crushed

1 teaspoon caraway seeds

3 cloves garlic, minced

Chili powder

Melt the butter in a large saucepan over medium-high heat. Add the beer, black currants, and rhubarb. Bring to a boil. Stir in the salt. Reduce the heat to simmer.

Add the juniper berries, thyme, rosemary, and caraway seeds. Simmer for 1 hour.

Add the garlic and chili powder to taste. The amount depends on the chili blend you use. Jaan adds it until he begins to feel the heat coming from the back of his mouth a few seconds after tasting.

You can finish the mop in two different styles: "jerk style," leaving all the solid ingredients in the mop, and "gourmet style," strained through a sieve.

Use the mop to baste your meat while cooking and reserve a little for serving too.

BBQ Freaks Rum-Guava Barbecue Sauce

Makes about 8 cups

Here's a sauce from the BBQ Freaks that will get your guests' attention. Although it contains ketchup, the most often used ingredient in barbecue sauces today, the rum and guava paste yield a flavor profile that says, "This is really different and really good!" We like it on almost anything, but especially on grilled beef or pork burgers, pulled pork, brats, and pork chops.

21 ounces guava paste (see Note)

2 cups ketchup

½ cup apple cider vinegar

1 cup good-quality rum

½ cup Worcestershire sauce

¼ cup molasses

¼ cup prepared yellow mustard

2 tablespoons Liquid Smoke

1 cup packed brown sugar

¼ cup of your favorite barbecue seasoning

In a food processor, blend together the guava paste, ketchup, and cider vinegar until smooth. Set aside.

In a heavy-bottomed saucepan over medium heat, combine the rum, Worcestershire, molasses, mustard, Liquid Smoke, brown sugar, and barbecue seasoning and whisk well. Add the guava mixture to the rum mixture and mix well. Simmer, stirring occasionally, for at least 30 minutes before serving.

Note: Guava paste is available in the Hispanic section of your supermarket or at gourmet specialty stores.

Dirty Dick's Barbecue Sauce

Makes about 4 cups

Here Richard Westhaver (see page 147) goes again, sharing some secrets. This sauce contains some standard ingredients found in many other sauces, but the amount he uses and what Dirty Dick does with it is what makes the sauce unique and outstanding. It could become the condiment of choice at your backyard barbecues, whether you're serving hot dogs, brats, burgers, butts, or brisket. We haven't tried it on seafood yet, but why not?

4 tablespoons (½ stick) butter

1 medium yellow onion, finely chopped

½ red bell pepper, cored, seeded, and diced

2 tablespoons minced garlic

3 cups ketchup

½ cup molasses

2 tablespoons hot sauce

¼ cup grainy mustard

3 tablespoons balsamic vinegar

½ cup packed brown sugar

3 tablespoons Worcestershire sauce

Juice of 1 lemon

2 tablespoons Dirty Dick's
Barbecue Spice (page 147)

Salt and freshly ground black pepper

Melt the butter in saucepan over medium-high heat. Add the onion, red bell pepper, and garlic and sauté until the onion is soft. Add the ketchup, molasses, hot sauce, mustard, vinegar, brown sugar, Worcestershire, lemon juice, and spice and simmer for 1 to 2 hours. Season to taste with salt and pepper just before serving.

Craig Whitson's Voodoo Butter

Makes about 2½ cups

Craig (see page 125) likes to use his voodoo butter (inspired by some Frank Zappa lyrics) to enhance pasta, potatoes, or rice. In fact, he heaps it on almost anything except ice cream, cake, or pie. Some of his other favorite foods to pair with this butter are fresh mussels steamed on the grill (see photo), all grilled meats—especially chicken and beef or pork steaks—fish, and all vegetables, grilled or steamed. He recommends making it ahead of time and storing it in the freezer so your voodoo sauce is "never more than a slice away!"

1 cup (2 sticks) unsalted butter, at room temperature

3 canned chipotle chiles, finely chopped

4 cloves garlic, minced

1 tablespoon packed brown sugar

½ teaspoon freshly ground black pepper

Grated zest of ½ orange

3 tablespoons freshly squeezed orange juice

Salt

Place the butter, chipotles, garlic, brown sugar, pepper, orange zest, orange juice, and salt to taste in a medium mixing bowl. Mix well with an electric mixer.

Transfer the mixture to a piece of plastic wrap and form it into a thick, sausagelike roll. Wrap it in the plastic and freeze until ready to use. Slice off pieces as needed.

Bonnie Q Grilled Pineapple Peach Salsa

Makes about 2 cups

When Doug Pierce develops a new recipe, he tests it until it is perfect. He tested this one four times. We tested it once, and have repeated it often since, by popular demand. Although Doug's original use for this salsa was as a topping for grilled pork chops, we have served it on chopped barbecue pork butt, grilled brats, barbecue bologna, and other meats with great results. It also stands alone as an outstanding dip with tortilla chips. The sweetness from grilled pineapple and peaches, contrasted with sour lime juice, peppers, and cilantro, imparts a signature flavor that brings smiles to to your guests' faces. You may want to double the quantity after your first go-around with it.

½ **fresh pineapple, peeled, cored, and cut into 1-inch slices**

2 **fresh peaches, pitted and quartered, or frozen peach slices**

1 **poblano chile or 3 jalapeños if you want more heat, seeded and diced**

½ **red bell pepper, cored, seeded, and diced**

¼ **cup coarsely chopped fresh cilantro**

Juice of 2 limes

Pinch of salt

Prepare a hot grill.

Lightly oil the grates and place the pineapple on it, followed by the peaches, cut side down. Cook until they develop good grill marks and the sugars in the fruit begin to caramelize. Set aside to cool on a plate or in a pan so you can reserve any juice to add to the finished salsa.

In a medium mixing bowl, combine the chiles, bell pepper, cilantro, lime juice, and salt. Dice the pineapple and peaches and add them to the bowl. Mix well, then taste and adjust the salt.

Julie "Da Boss"'s Margaritas

Serves 4

We don't know when and how it happened, but when Doug Pierce (see below), his daughter Bonnie, and Julie Willing decided to team up for their Bonnie Q BBQ catering and roadhouse business, they opened a new chapter in barbecue history. The lucky folks who live near Dillon, Colorado, or who visit for skiing and other outdoor recreation are so taken with Bonnie Q's barbecue that there could be a whole book of many chapters in the works. What better way to celebrate the founding and phenomenal success of Bonnie Q BBQ—or any other happy occasion in your backyard—than with Julie's special refreshing margaritas? Cheers to Doug, Bonnie, excellence in barbecue, and "Da Boss"!

1 cup silver tequila (100% agave)

¼ cup orange liqueur, such as Cointreau or Triple Sec

1 tablespoon agave nectar

¾ cup orange juice

½ cup limeade or freshly squeezed lime juice

¼ cup water

Salt, for the glasses (optional)

Orange and lime wedges, for garnish (optional)

Combine the tequila, orange liqueur, juices, and water in a shaker with ice or blend with ice for frozen margaritas. Serve in margarita or martini glasses, rimmed with salt if desired. Garnish with a wedge of orange and lime if desired.

DOUG PIERCE, BONNIE Q BBQ

I got involved in competition barbecue 20 years ago quite by accident. A friend borrowed our Ole Hickory Pit Smoker from the resort where I was a chef to compete in Frisco, Colorado (the year before it became a Kansas City Barbeque Society–sanctioned event). I had nothing better to do that Saturday, so I stopped by to check it out. My friend was in the weeds selling 'que, so I jumped in to help out. I had a great time, and the rest is history. We competed the following year, and I have every year since.

CHAPTER 7: When you've eaten your way through this chapter you'll never again think—if you ever mistakenly did—that championship barbecuers live, breathe, cook, and eat only meat. The recipes we selected for this chapter run the gamut from easy to complex and light to robust. As with the recipes in other chapters, some are prepared indoors, some outdoors, and some both indoors and out. All are served by our champions in their own backyards.

All who knew Big Will Wright of Topeka, Kansas, still mourn his untimely death. As a fond remembrance of and tribute to him, we have shared the famous cheesecake recipe that he donated for the *Kansas City Barbeque Society Cookbook, 25th Anniversary Edition*. The recipe is introduced with recollections shared by Marty Lynch, Big Will's barbecue cooking contest teammate.

We can't imagine a barbecue cookbook without a fruit salad. It's a cool, refreshing ending to a big meal on a warm summer night. So, due to popular demand from the *Kansas City Barbeque Society Cookbook, 25th Anniversary Edition*, Rosemary Morrow, of AM & PM Smokers, gave us her recipe. Likewise, for most barbecue champs, fruit cobbler is always on the Top-10 favorites list. We guarantee that when you taste Paul Schatte's peach cobbler you'll know why!

To add citrusy zest to your backyard barbecue, we recommend Que's Your Daddy Triple-Layer Lemon Cake. When life gives you lemons, make this cake instead of lemonade!

Thanks to Rich and Bunny Tuttle, you can surprise your guests with a dessert that is likely to be a totally new surprise: Blueberry Wontons.

You might be surprised to see that dessert can be cooked on a grill, but once you've tried Chef Paul's Fluffy Turtles and grilled pound cake, you may never go back to baking. As an added bonus, the dessert chef can stay outside where the action is.

Get ready to wow yourself and your guests. These dishes are good enough to merit an outdoor party on their own!

Desserts

Big Will's Triple-Chocolate Cheesecake

Makes 1 (9-inch) cheesecake

Big Will was a professional chef who excelled in life as well as the kitchen. He didn't just talk the Golden Rule; he exemplified it. And his culinary creations were so delicious that they were acts of kindness for body and soul. When Big Will said, "I'll bring cheesecake to the barbecue," we smiled in anticipation. His cheesecakes were always over the top in quality and flavor. It doesn't surprise us at all that the very first time he entered this Triple-Chocolate Cheesecake in the dessert category at the American Royal Open, it got a perfect 180. His teammate Marty told us, "When they called our team name to come up and claim First Place in Dessert, Will yelled 'YES' and floated up to the stage!" Treat yourself to a taste of barbecue history, kindness, and one of the best cheesecakes you'll ever serve in your backyard or anywhere else!

CRUST

3 cups Oreo cookie crumbs

¼ cup sugar

8 tablespoons (1 stick) butter, melted

FILLING

3 (8-ounce) packages Philadelphia cream cheese (don't skimp), softened

1 (8-ounce) package mascarpone cheese, softened

2 (14-ounce) cans Eagle brand sweetened condensed milk

1 cup Hershey's chocolate syrup

1 cup Hershey's unsweetened cocoa powder

½ cup Ovaltine mix

1 cup sugar

2 tablespoons vanilla extract

3 large eggs

WILLIAM WRIGHT, WILL DEAL CATERING AND BBQ COMPANY

The barbecue world lost Big Will to heart failure on April 29, 2010. As a tribute to him, we pulled this from the *Kansas City Barbeque Society Cookbook, 25th Anniversary Edition*, which was released a few days after his death. We are using it with permission because it brings back so many memories that we just had to include it here.

Preheat the oven to 350°F. To make the crust, combine the cookie crumbs, sugar, and melted butter in a large bowl and mix with your hands until the cookie crumbs start to get sticky, then press the mixture into the bottom of a 9-inch springform pan or silicone cake pan. Bake for 10 minutes; remove from the oven and cool on a wire rack.

Reduce the oven temperature to 300°F. To make the filling, place the cream cheese and mascarpone cheese in a stand mixer fitted with a paddle attachment and mix until smooth. Add the sweetened condensed milk, chocolate syrup, cocoa powder, Ovaltine, sugar, and vanilla; mix until incorporated. Add the eggs, one at a time, incorporating each one thoroughly before adding another. Mix for 10 minutes at low speed, scraping the bowl often. Pour the filling into the pan and bake for 1 hour and 20 minutes.

Turn off the oven, but let the pan cool in the oven for 1 hour. After the cheesecake cools, place it in the freezer to chill for at least 4 hours or overnight. Remove the cheesecake from the pan while frozen and allow it to sit for 20 minutes before slicing.

Rosemary's Fruit Salad

Serves 10 to 12

Rosemary Morrow, of AM & PM Smokers (page 57), is Phil Morrow's wife and partner for life. This easy, delicious combination of peach, pineapple, Mandarin oranges, strawberries, and bananas is never left begging at the end of the Morrows' backyard barbecues, even when everyone has eaten so much barbecue that they thought they couldn't possibly eat another bite of anything. Rosemary always proves them wrong!

1 (21-ounce) can peach pie filling

1 (20-ounce) can pineapple chunks, drained

1 (11-ounce) can Mandarin oranges, drained

1 (16-ounce) package frozen strawberries or fresh strawberries (about 1 cup sliced)

2 medium bananas

In a large serving bowl, combine the peach pie filling, pineapple chunks, mandarin oranges, and strawberries; mix well and refrigerate overnight. Right before serving, slice the bananas, add them to the mix, and stir.

Paul Schatte's Head Country II Peach Cobbler

Serves 8

The first dish that comes to mind when nine out of ten barbecuers hear the word dessert is fruit cobbler, and peach cobbler is always a favorite. Easy to fix and ever a hit at a backyard barbecue. "This dessert will be the ultimate complement to any homestyle barbecue meal," Paul (see page 29) assured us. We tried it, and we heartily agree!

2 cups fresh peaches, peeled, pitted, and cut into wedges

4 tablespoons (½ stick) butter

1 cup all-purpose flour

1 cup sugar

1 teaspoon baking powder

1 teaspoon vanilla extract

¾ cup milk

Vanilla ice cream, for serving

Preheat a smoker or oven to 350°F.

When cooking on the smoker, Paul likes to use a cast-iron skillet. You can also use an aluminum pan. Preheat the skillet, then lay the peaches in the skillet.

Melt the butter in a 1- or 1½-quart saucepan. In a medium mixing bowl, combine the flour, sugar, baking powder, vanilla, and milk and stir to make a batter. Pour the batter into the melted butter, but do not stir. Pour this mixture directly over the fruit—again do not stir. Cover the pan with foil and cook for 1 to 1¼ hours. After 1 hour, check with a toothpick to see if it comes out clean. If not, cook for 15 minutes more, or until done. Top with vanilla ice cream.

Que's Your Daddy Triple-Layer Lemon Cake

Makes 1 (8-inch) round 3-layer cake, serves 12

The lemon curd filling and light lemon cream cheese frosting make this three-layer cake from Que's Your Daddy burst with flavor. You can use a decorator tip to add a fancy touch to the frosting or simply garnish it with slices of fresh lemon. Either way, it's a summertime favorite, great for special occasions!

LEMON CURD

3 large egg yolks, lightly beaten

½ cup granulated sugar

1 tablespoon cornstarch

1½ teaspoons finely grated lemon zest

3 tablespoons freshly squeezed lemon juice

3 tablespoons water

4 tablespoons (½ stick) butter, softened and cut into small chunks

CAKE

2⅓ cups all-purpose flour

1½ teaspoons baking powder

½ teaspoon baking soda

¼ teaspoon salt

1 cup (2 sticks) butter, at room temperature

2 cups sugar

1 tablespoon finely grated lemon zest

2 tablespoons freshly squeezed lemon juice

4 large eggs

1 cup buttermilk

FROSTING

2 (3-ounce) packages cream cheese, softened

8 tablespoons (½ stick) butter, at room temperature

2 teaspoons freshly squeezed lemon juice

4½ to 4¾ cups confectioners' sugar

2 teaspoons finely grated lemon zest

Make the lemon curd: Place the egg yolks in a medium mixing bowl and set aside. In a small saucepan over medium heat, combine the sugar and cornstarch. Stir in the zest, juice, and water. Cook and stir until thickened and bubbly. Gradually stir about half of the hot lemon mixture into the egg yolks, working slowly so the eggs don't cook enough to scramble. Return the egg yolk mixture to the saucepan. Cook and stir over medium heat until the mixture comes to a gentle boil. Cook and stir for 2 minutes more. Stir in the butter until melted. Remove from the heat. Transfer to a bowl, cover the surface with plastic wrap, and chill for 1 hour.

Make the cake: Preheat your cooker (or oven) to 350°F. Grease and lightly flour three 8-inch round cake pans; set aside.

In a medium bowl, stir together the flour, baking powder, baking soda, and salt; set aside. In a large bowl, beat the butter with an electric mixer on medium to high speed for 30 seconds. Add the sugar, zest, and juice and beat until com-

bined, scraping the sides of the bowl occasionally. Add the eggs, one at a time, beating well after each addition. Alternatively add the flour mixture and buttermilk, beating on low speed after each addition just until combined. Pour the batter into the prepared pans, spreading evenly. Bake for 28 to 32 minutes, or until a toothpick inserted near the center comes out clean. Cool in the pans on wire racks for 10 minutes. Remove from the pans and cool completely on the racks.

Make the frosting: In a medium mixing bowl, combine the cream cheese, butter, and lemon juice. Beat with an electric mixer on low to medium speed until light and fluffy. Gradually add the confectioners' sugar, beating until the frosting is of spreading consistency. Stir in the zest.

To assemble: Turn 2 cake layers bottom side up and spread each with lemon curd. Place the third layer bottom side up on a serving plate. Turn one layer with lemon curd over and stack it curd side down on the plated layer. Repeat with the top layer, curd side down. Frost the top and sides.

Who Are Those Guys? Smoked Pecan Squares

Makes 16

A recipe by Barefoot Contessa Ina Garten was George's original inspiration for this recipe. He has made it many times in his home oven, as well as his barbecue smoker, with great success. He told us that his guests like it best when the pecan squares are smoked. Sometimes he smokes extra pecans to sprinkle on top and to store in an airtight container for enjoying on top of ice cream.

CRUST

2½ cups (5 sticks) unsalted butter,
   at room temperature

¾ cup granulated sugar

3 large eggs

¾ teaspoon vanilla extract

4½ cups all-purpose flour

¼ teaspoon sea salt

½ teaspoon baking powder

TOPPING

2 cups (4 sticks) unsalted butter

½ cup honey

½ cup maple syrup

3 cups firmly packed brown sugar

1 teaspoon grated lemon zest

1 teaspoon grated orange zest

2 pounds chopped pecans (see Notes)

¼ cup heavy cream

Preheat your smoker (or oven) to 350°F. Lightly butter a 9 by 12-inch aluminum pan (i.e., a half pan).

Make the crust: Beat the butter and sugar with an electric mixer on medium speed until fluffy, 2 to 3 minutes. With the mixer running, add the eggs, one at a time, and the vanilla and mix well.

Sift the flour, salt, and baking powder together, then add them to the batter and beat with the mixer on low speed until just mixed. Dump the mixture into the prepared pan. The batter will be very sticky. Press the mixture into the bottom of the pan. It helps to lightly sprinkle your hands and the top of the batter with flour. Bake for 15 minutes, or until the crust is hardened but not brown. Let cool, but leave the smoker or oven at 350°F.

Make the topping: Combine the butter, honey, maple syrup, brown sugar, and both zests in a large cast-iron skillet. Heat over low heat until the butter melts and the ingredients are combined, stirring often with a wooden spoon. Increase the heat and let boil for 3 minutes, stirring often. Remove from the heat, add the pecans, and gently stir in the cream.

Pour the filling over the crust, smooth it out, and bake for 25 to 30 minutes, or until the filling is set. Let cool completely in the pan.

Cover and chill, then cut into squares and serve.

GEORGE HENSLER, WHO ARE THOSE GUYS?

Who Are Those Guys? is a group of 5 friends who enjoy each other's company and are always looking for a good excuse to get together, burn some meat, and drink a few cold, tasty beverages. Cooking at a barbecue competition proved to be a perfect venue for their shenanigans. During their first 3 years on the competition circuit, the gang surprised many, including themselves. They learned a lot, improved their methods, met a lot of fine folks, and made more than a few very good friends—all while having some fun and eating some tasty barbecue from time to time. Cooking a total of 18 contests in their first 3 years, the team received a total of 35 calls to the stage. Their awards have included first-place calls in ribs, chicken, and brisket, as well as 3 reserves and 1 grand championship.

Notes: For an interesting variation, try using walnuts or a mix of pecans and walnuts. Peanuts work well too.

You can drizzle the squares with chocolate or caramel after plating to gussy them up, or you can even try dipping half the square into a mix of melted chocolate.

Wrapped tightly in plastic wrap, the squares will keep for a week or so in the refrigerator.

The Baron's Grilled Pound Cake with Sour Cherry and Pecan Ice Cream

Serves 8

Chef Paul comes from a big family—five sisters and a brother, besides Paul. They get together for all of the holidays and several times during the summer. This is one of his family's favorite desserts for summer get-togethers. P.S. He cut down the recipes for you; they usually make at least three pound cakes at a time!

¾ cup dried sour cherries

1 cup boiling water

1½ pints vanilla ice cream, slightly softened

Heaping ¼ cup coarsely chopped semisweet chocolate

⅓ cup pecans, toasted and coarsely chopped

1 (1-pound) loaf pound cake

4 tablespoons (½ stick) unsalted butter, melted

¼ cup brandy

Place the cherries in a medium bowl. Pour the boiling water over them and set aside until softened, about 10 minutes. Drain; pat dry.

Place the ice cream in a large bowl. Mix in the cherries, semisweet chocolate, and pecans. Cover and freeze until firm, about 2 hours.

Heat a grill to medium. Cut the pound cake into 16 ½-inch slices. Brush both sides of each cake slice with melted butter. Grill the slices until lightly toasted, about 30 seconds per side. Place 2 cake slices each on 8 dessert plates. Place 1 scoop of ice cream atop each plate of cake slices. Drizzle 1½ teaspoons of brandy over each serving.

Marty Lynch's Gaelic Cream

Serves 2 to 4, depending on your level of thirst

You can start a new after-dinner tradition with an Irish accent when you serve this Gaelic Cream from Marty (see page 83) after a barbecue feast in your backyard. It's a perfect sweet ending to a memorable meal.

1 (14-ounce) can sweetened
   condensed milk

1½ cups heavy cream

4½ teaspoons chocolate syrup

¾ cup Irish (or other) whiskey

In a blender, combine all the ingredients and blend on medium speed until thoroughly mixed. Cover and refrigerate until ready to serve, then mix again and serve over ice.

The Baron's Fluffy Turtles

Makes 24 to 48 pieces

This recipe evolved from the classic fluffernutters. You might think it's for the kids, but you'll be surprised by how many adults you'll have to fight off so there are enough for the kids. While technically they don't include pecans, we still like to call them Fluffy Turtles.

12 (10-inch) flour tortillas

1 (16-ounce) jar plain peanut butter

2 (7- to 7½-ounce) jars Marshmallow Fluff

High-heat cooking spray

1 (12-ounce) package mini chocolate chips

½ cup chopped pecans

1 (20-ounce) jar caramel sauce (see Note)

Preheat your grill to medium-hot.

Spread 6 of the tortillas with peanut butter and the other 6 tortillas with Marshmallow Fluff.

Spray the grill with high-heat cooking spray or use tongs to rub a clean cloth coated with vegetable oil over the grates. Place one of each of the tortillas, peanut butter or Fluff up, on the grill. Don't try to do more. Heat until warm, 2 to 3 minutes. Sprinkle with chocolate chips and pecans, and drizzle with caramel sauce on the peanut butter side. Flip the marshmallow tortillas on top of the peanut butter tortillas.

Set aside on a cutting board to cool. Repeat with the remaining tortillas. Cut the cooled Fluffy Turtles into quarters or eighths, as desired, and serve.

Note: We prefer Smucker's squeezable caramel topping over any of the others out there, but by all means use your favorite. We also use homemade, which is even better if you want to go to the trouble.

KCass Blueberry Wontons

Serves 8 to 10

Nothing says summer like fresh blueberries. If a pie seems like too much trouble, these easy blueberry wontons will be a popular dessert option at your house from now on. Rich and Bunny adapted this filling from one they got from Chef Paul. It is always a huge hit at their annual Tamale Party and backyard barbecues.

FILLING

1 (8-ounce) package cream cheese, softened

½ cup crushed fresh blueberries

1 (1-pound) package wonton wrappers (24 to 36)

1 to 2 tablespoons confectioners' sugar

Fresh blueberries, for topping

Preheat the oven to 350°F or heat a grill to the same temperature for indirect cooking. Coat a baking sheet (or 9 by 12-inch aluminum pan, or half pan) with nonstick cooking spray.

Place the cream cheese and crushed blueberries in a medium bowl and mix well.

Place a little of the filling in the center of each wonton wrapper and fold up (crab rangoon style) to cover the filling. Place the filled wontons about 2 inches apart on the prepared pan. Bake until they start to brown, about 10 minutes.

Let cool, then sprinkle with confectioners' sugar and blueberries before serving.

Seriously BBQ Tongue-Melting Chocolate Parfait

Serves 6 to 8

Jeremy's chocolate parfait does more than melt on your tongue. The chocolate, blended with egg yolks, butter, cream, and a quality liqueur, will have your guests wishing they had saved more room for dessert. This dessert is perfect at home, at a formal banquet, or at a backyard barbecue. If it seems too formal for your party, serve it in individual small canning jars. Note: The eggs are not cooked enough to pass muster with the U.S. FDA. You can substitute pasteurized eggs to be totally safe.

8 ounces chocolate (60 to 70 percent cocoa)

4 large egg yolks

4 tablespoons (½ stick) unsalted butter, melted

1¼ cups heavy whipping cream

2 teaspoons vanilla extract

2 teaspoons of your favorite liqueur, such as Grand Marnier or Armagnac

Melt the chocolate in the top of a double boiler. Set aside.

In a medium bowl, beat the egg yolks, then gently add the melted butter. Fold in the melted chocolate. Chill for at least 1 hour before serving.

In a medium mixing bowl, combine the cream, vanilla, and liqueur. Whip with an electric mixer on medium speed until soft peaks form.

Layer the chocolate and whipped cream in serving dishes or parfait glasses.

Our first debt of gratitude goes to the barbecue champs who responded to our call for recipes and other information. We asked many champs for a lot of information. The ones you see in this book responded to the call, and you are the beneficiary. We appreciate the good intentions of many who intended to respond but for business or other reasons couldn't get to it in time for our deadlines. We understand, and we hope to work with you on future books.

It was truly a delight to be in contact with so many barbecue champs as we wrote this book. We learned more about them, more about us, and more about barbecue. We give them our hearty thanks! Not only have they given you some top-notch recipes to ramp up your future backyard barbecues; they have reaffirmed for us that the spirit of cooperation and sharing is still alive and well in the competition barbecue community.

We thank the many deceased barbecue champs and friends upon whose shoulders today's pitmasters stand. Although their physical presence is gone, their influence and spirit remain. We are better persons and cooks for having known them. We especially want to single out Gary Wells, Al Lawson, Karen Putnam, Tony Stone, Big Will Wright, Bob Carruthers, Fred Gould, Brian Heinecke, Cheryl Litman, Jack Kay, Cliff Weddington, Maxine "Shaky Puddin" Fiel, Jimmy Bedford, Judy Heslar, Don Gillis, Charlie Vergos, Ray "Red" Gil, Charlie Knote, Raymond Robinson, Otis Boyd, Arthur Bryant, Andrea Ravinett Martin, Jim Quessenberry, Herb Schwartz, Bobby Mueller, Pete Jones, and Giancarlo Giannelli.

Thanks to our many friends in the barbecue industry who sustain us with their barbecue and carry the barbecue tradition forward to today's and tomorrow's generations. To name only a few: Dr. Rich Davis, Jack Fiorella, Case Dorman, Johnny White, Ron Quick, Jeff & Joy Stehney, Doug Worgul, Josh Johnston, Eric White, A. D. Chappell, Phil Donaldson, DennyMike Sherman, Ben Lang, Brad Barrett, Don McLemore, Van Sykes, Josh Baum, Otis & Earlene Walker, Nicole Davenport, John Markus, Wilbur King, Lindsay Shannon, Ryan Brooks, Edgar, Norma, Kent & Buddy Black, Kelly & Roni Wertz, Amy Anderson, Melanie Tapia, Elaine Anton, Curtis Tuff, Mike Mills, Amy Mills, John Stage, Danny & Carey Head, John "Daredevil Bad McFad" Raven, Wayne Mueller, Joe Don Davidson, Jack Cawthon, Ray Green, Bill Felder, Dave & Lynn Aronson, Danny Meyers, Silky & Joellyn Sullivan, Sandra Lyon, David Bailey, Carl Rothrock, Mike & Debbie McMillan, Dr. Howard Taylor, Melvin & Maurice Bessinger, John T Edge, Matt & Ted Lee, Ed Mitchell, Ron Harwell, Mike & Theresa Lake, Charlotte Finch, Scott McClard, Danny & Carolyn Gaulden, Adam Perry Lang, David Campbell,

Acknowledgments

Mark Brown, Frank Alfonso, Velmer Stevenson, Joel Latham, Moses Quartey, Jerry Vandergrift, Wilber Shirley, Elizabeth Lumpkin, Rusty "Rooster" Dees, Rudy Mikeska, Washington Perry, Jeff Sanders, Steve & Janice Katz, Mike & Audrey Budai, Carolyn Wells, Wayne Lohman, Bill Gage, Randy Bigler, Tana Shupe, Debbie Christian, Marge Plummer, Chris Marks, Bob Snelson, Mike & Debbie Davis, Rod Gray, Myron Mixon, Anne Rehnstrom, Kathie Dakai, Guy "Guido" Fieri, Guido & Cathy Meindl, Michael McDearman, Ardith & Ted Richardson, Don & Leslie Lovely, Tom & Lisa Raitt, Kathleen McIntosh, Jay "The Snail" Vantuyl, Monty Spradling, Mike Tucker, Tuffy Stone, Johnny Trigg, George Hensler, Olivia & Sonny Ashford, Nick Spinelli, Mike Garrison, Jerry Bressel & the entire Flying BBQ Judges planeload!

It isn't a mystery to friends who know him that Ardie loves to read mysteries. He was a loyal customer at the former I Love a Mystery bookstore in Mission, Kansas. That connection led to mention of the barbecue mystery genre in *The Kansas City Barbeque Society Cookbook, 25th Anniversary Edition*. The store sponsored several book-signing events for us, complete with free barbecue samples from nearby Johnny's Bar-B-Cue. Hats off to the I Love a Mystery staff: Becci West, Maggie Wood, Lou Pieper, Louise Lucas, and Toni Bennington.

Special thanks to Mary, Gretchen, Jessica, Chris, Erin, Sarah, Alan, Zachary, Henry, Emma, Lee, Kelli, Elliott, Elise, and Todd for their love and encouragement and for tolerating our absence because "the book is almost due!" all along the way.

Thanks also for encouragement and ideas from friends—Gloria Walker, Linda Ray, Stan & Ann Nelson, Phyllis Mueller, Perry and Cheri Skrukrud, Ron and Joan Goettsch, Bill Herman, Ron, Mary & Geof Buchholz, Terry Lee, Diane Thompson, George Dugger, Mary Winslow, Howard Rasmussen, Sherry Melberg, Becky Bryant, Jerry & Diane Wilson, Mark & Tammy Almich, and Jill Schwiderski.

We are again thankful for quiet meeting space in the Cedar Roe Library, Roeland Park, Kansas. Thanks to friendly, competent, resourceful staffers Meredith Roberson, branch manager, and Michele Holden for making space available for us. We applaud the work of the entire staff at Cedar Roe Library for making it a valuable community resource for patrons of all ages. A tip of our hats to former library staffer Debbie Crough, wishing you a happy retirement.

We are forever grateful for and proud to work with the outstanding team of professionals at Andrews McMeel Publishing. Our special thanks to Kirsty Melville, head of the book division, for adopting us as her barbecue guys; Lane Butler, our super-competent editor, who keeps us on task, is attentive to details, is a gentle, patient taskmaster, and makes us look good. Tim Lynch and Diane Marsh, the design team, embellish our text with artful, appealing photos and graphic eye candy from cover to cover. Emily Farris, our publicist, spreads the word about our books far and wide. Lynn McAdoo, and everyone else in sales, works with book vendors large and small to make sure we're out front and visible.

Dennis Hayes, our friend, advocate, and agent, is always several steps ahead, navigating us through the exciting changes in today's publishing industry, one project at a time.

Finally, we thank Scott Turow, president of the Authors Guild, and the excellent guild staff for helping us with contract details, keeping us informed of publishing industry issues vital to authors' well-being, and their continuous advocacy for all authors.

PHOTO CREDITS

Most images were provided by the authors. The following people contributed additional images.

Clint Cantwell: 2 (right), 4, 50 (bottom), 77 (left)

Paul Schatte: 10, 29 (middle), 58, 161 (left)

Danielle Dimovski: 14 (far left), 118, 119

Burt Culver: 16 (bottom left), 37

Eddie Tonino and Frank Kondor: 19, 41

Bruce and Lin Langseth: 21

Jeff Brown: 27, 49

Bob and Donna Oldfield: 24 (top right), 35 (left), 135

Kelly and Roni Wertz: 35 (right), 45, 138

Jason and Megan Day: 38

Jeremy Fowler: 40, 170

Michelle Taft: 43

Scott and Suzanne Burton: 47

Smoky Jon Olson: 48

Dan Hixon: 52

Jose Bengoa, Yolanda Bolivar, and Gabriel Antunez: 55, 130 (right), 131

Phil and Rosemary Morrow: 57 (top)

Tim and Wendy Boucher: 59

Rick Naug: 63, 122

Hector Rivera: 65

Tim Lynch: 72 (right), 126 (bottom right)

Mike and Beth Wozniak: 68, 69

Mike and Scott Cook: 73

Chris Lilly: 75 (top)

Steve Renfro: 80, 81

Rich and Bunny Tuttle: 85, 169

Joel and Erin Matteson: 90

Tom and Michele Perelka: 94, 132

Bob Fite and Steve Blake: 95

Jaan Habicht: 96, 97, 130 (left), 150 (left)

Harry Soo: 103

Bill Minahan: 104, 107

Chris Capell: 108 (top), 109

Jim Erickson: 111, 121 (left)

DennyMike Sherman: 113 (left)

Bill Gillespie: 115

Scottie Johnson: 116

Craig Whitson: 125 (left, top, middle), 134, 153

Darian and Jamie Khosravi: 137

Richard Westhaver: 148, 152 (left)

Doug Pierce: 154, 155

Christian Foster and Lane Butler: 160 (left), 166, 167 (right), 168

Doc and Susan Richardson: 162, 163

George Hensler: 165

Metric Conversions

Approximate Metric Equivalents

VOLUME

¼ teaspoon	1 milliliter
½ teaspoon	2.5 milliliters
¾ teaspoon	4 milliliters
1 teaspoon	5 milliliters
1¼ teaspoons	6 milliliters
1½ teaspoons	7.5 milliliters
1¾ teaspoons	8.5 milliliters
2 teaspoons	10 milliliters
1 tablespoon (½ fluid ounce)	15 milliliters
2 tablespoons (1 fluid ounce)	30 milliliters
¼ cup	60 milliliters
⅓ cup	80 milliliters
½ cup (4 fluid ounces)	120 milliliters
⅔ cup	160 milliliters
¾ cup	180 milliliters
1 cup (8 fluid ounces)	240 milliliters
1¼ cups	300 milliliters
1½ cups (12 fluid ounces)	360 milliliters
1⅔ cups	400 milliliters
2 cups (1 pint)	460 milliliters
3 cups	700 milliliters
4 cups (1 quart)	0.95 liter
1 quart plus ¼ cup	1 liter
4 quarts (1 gallon)	3.8 liters

LENGTH

⅛ inch	3 millimeters
¼ inch	6 millimeters
½ inch	1.25 centimeters
1 inch	2.5 centimeters
2 inches	5 centimeters
2½ inches	6 centimeters
4 inches	10 centimeters
5 inches	13 centimeters
6 inches	15.25 centimeters
12 inches (1 foot)	30 centimeters

WEIGHT

¼ ounce	7 grams
½ ounce	14 grams
¾ ounce	21 grams
1 ounce	28 grams
1¼ ounces	35 grams
1½ ounces	42.5 grams
1⅔ ounces	45 grams
2 ounces	57 grams
3 ounces	85 grams
4 ounces (¼ pound)	113 grams
5 ounces	142 grams
6 ounces	170 grams
7 ounces	198 grams
8 ounces (½ pound)	227 grams
16 ounces (1 pound)	454 grams
35.25 ounces (2.2 pounds)	1 kilogram

Metric Conversion Formulas

TO CONVERT	MULTIPLY
Ounces to grams	Ounces by 28.35
Pounds to kilograms	Pounds by 0.454
Teaspoons to milliliters	Teaspoons by 4.93
Tablespoons to milliliters	Tablespoons by 14.79
Fluid ounces to milliliters	Fluid ounces by 29.57
Cups to milliliters	Cups by 236.59
Cups to liters	Cups by 0.236
Pints to liters	Pints by 0.473
Quarts to liters	Quarts by 0.946
Gallons to liters	Gallons by 3.785
Inches to centimeters	Inches by 2.54

and Equivalents

Oven Temperatures

To convert Fahrenheit to Celsius, subtract 32 from Fahrenheit, multiply the result by 5, then divide by 9.

DESCRIPTION	FAHRENHEIT	CELSIUS	BRITISH GAS MARK
Very cool	200°	95°	0
Very cool	225°	110°	¼
Very cool	250°	120°	½
Cool	275°	135°	1
Cool	300°	150°	2
Warm	325°	165°	3
Moderate	350°	175°	4
Moderately hot	375°	190°	5
Fairly hot	400°	200°	6
Hot	425°	220°	7
Very hot	450°	230°	8
Very hot	475°	245°	9

Common Ingredients and Their Approximate Equivalents

1 cup uncooked rice = 225 grams

1 cup all-purpose flour = 140 grams

1 stick butter (4 ounces • ½ cup • 8 tablespoons) = 110 grams

1 cup butter (8 ounces • 2 sticks • 16 tablespoons) = 220 grams

1 cup brown sugar, firmly packed = 225 grams

1 cup granulated sugar = 200 grams

Information compiled from a variety of sources, including *Recipes into Type* by Joan Whitman and Dolores Simon (Newton, MA: Biscuit Books, 2000); *The New Food Lover's Companion* by Sharon Tyler Herbst (Hauppauge, NY: Barron's, 1995); and *Rosemary Brown's Big Kitchen Instruction Book* (Kansas City, MO: Andrews McMeel, 1998).

INDEX

ABOUT THE AUTHORS

Ardie A. Davis, also known as Remus Powers, Ph.B., founded the Diddy-Wa-Diddy National Barbecue Sauce Contest in his backyard patio in 1984. Three years later the contest became the American Royal International Barbecue Sauce, Rub & Baste Contest. A charter member of the Kansas City Barbeque Society (KCBS) and former three-term member of the KCBS Board of Directors, Ardie is now a board member emeritus, a Certified Master Judge, and an inductee in the KCBS Hall of Flame (1992). He is also a certified Memphis in May barbecue judge, and in 2008, he was a featured judge at the 20th Annual Jack Daniel's World Championship Invitational Barbecue in Lynchburg, Tennessee.

Ardie is a founder of Greasehouse University (1984) and serves as president, Diddy-Wa-Diddy Board of Barbecue at the university. He was interviewed and appeared in two History Channel shows: *Modern Marvels* and *America Eats*. Other shows he has appeared in include *How the States Got Their Shapes*, and *United Tastes of America* ("Kansas City Barbecue Festival") on the Cooking Channel. He is currently a freelance contributor for the *Kansas City Star* newspaper, the *Kansas City Bullsheet*, official newspaper of the Kansas City Barbeque Society (KCBS), and the *National Barbecue News*, which awarded him a Spirit of Barbecue Award in 2003 at the Jack Daniel's World Championship Invitational Barbecue. In 2002, he was presented with a Judges Choice Award at the Jack Daniel's World Championship Invitational Barbecue. Ardie's previous books include *The Great BBQ Sauce Book*, *Kansas City BBQ Pocket Guide*, *Techniques for Grilling*, and *Techniques for Smoking*.

Paul Kirk, aka Barbecue Guru, Ambassador of Barbecue, Order of the Magic Mop, Certified Master Barbecue Judge, member of the Kansas City Barbecue Society Board of Directors, and inductee into the Kansas City Barbeque Society Hall of Flame, has won more than 525 cooking and barbecue awards, among them seven world championships, including the prestigious American Royal Open, the world's largest BBQ contest.

For more than 12 years, Paul has operated the Baron's School of Pit Masters, teaching classes all over the world. He has also trained barbecue restaurant staffs across the United States and conducted seminars at national conventions for the International Association of Culinary Professionals (IACP). In 1998 and 2000, he was a member of the Julia Child BBQ Team of Ten at the IACP conventions, raising funds for the Julia Child Endowment Foundation.

Paul's previous books include *Paul Kirk's Championship Barbecue Sauces, Smokin', The Big Grill, Paul Kirk's Championship Barbecue,* and *500 Barbecue Bites*, and he is featured in a whole host of other barbecue cookbooks. He writes monthly columns for *Kansas City Bullsheet*, the *National Barbecue News*, and the *Goat Gap Gazette.* Paul has appeared on the *Today Show*, Discovery Channel, *CBS This Morning, Talk Soup,* and Anthony Bourdain's *In Search of the Perfect Meal.* He has been featured in the AARP's *Modern Maturity Magazine, Saveur,* and the *Calgary Herald.* He is a partner in Righteous Urban Barbecue (aka RUB) restaurants in New York City and Las Vegas. For more on Paul, visit www.baron-of-bbq.com.

The End